DONALDSON LINE

DONALDSON LINE
OF
GLASGOW

P. J. TELFORD

Opposite:
COLINA heading north east into
the Atlantic past Belle Isle
Painting by J. K. Byass

PUBLISHED BY THE WORLD SHIP SOCIETY
KENDAL LA9 7LT
1989

CONTENTS

Frontispiece		2
Foreword		5
Acknowledgements		6
Donaldson Line of Glasgow		7
Fleet List Notes		44
Fleet List:	Owned Ships	45
	Miscellaneous Craft owned or managed by Donaldson Line	92
	Ships managed on behalf of H.M. Government	93
Appendix 1	The Donaldson and Black Companies	98
	Dividend and Distribution Record 1953-1965	102
	Prices Paid for Ships	102
2	LETITIA (I)	103
3	CORRIENTES (I)	103
4	Grand Manan Island and the Bay of Fundy	105
5	Anticosti Island	107
6	CONCORDIA (II) and Sable Island	107
7	Loss of the TRITONIA (III)	108
8	The St. Lawrence Seaway System	111
9	CALGARIA	118
10	Chartered Tonnage	119
11	Flags and Funnels	120
12	LIVONIAN as a blockship at Dover	123
13	The Merchant Navy War Memorial	124
	The British Maritime Charitable Foundation "Memorial Book"	124
Fleet List Index		126

© P. J. Telford and World Ship Society, 28 Natland Road, Kendal
LA9 7LT England

ISBN Casebound edition 0 905617 54 1
Softback edition 0 905617 55 X

Printed by **Gibbons Barford Print**, Wolverhampton, England

FOREWORD

I would like to congratulate Mr. Telford on his excellent History of Ships of the Donaldson Line written for the World Ship Society. Having been Chief Officer in the company he would have had a lot of firsthand knowledge, but a great deal of research must have been required to trace the life of many of the ships, their different owners and flags under which they eventually sailed.

The original partnership which marked the beginning of the venture into shipping was really a family effort, from the early sailing ships and then into steam and was to continue throughout four generations until the company was put into voluntary liquidation, still largely family controlled.

With the vast changes which have taken place in shipping, it is difficult to imagine young men being able to venture into shipowning on their own today, just as it is difficult to contemplate that in these early days it was sometimes possible on one good voyage to leave enough profit to build another ship to add to the fleet.

To anyone interested in ships I feel sure they will find great interest and enjoyment in this book.

Kilbarchan, Signed: Fred A. Donaldson
Scotland.

Author's Note

Sadly, Mr. Fred Donaldson passed away in 1988. He was an employer highly respected by his staff and was from a class of shipowner not readily found in this era of impersonal management.

ACKNOWLEDGEMENTS

Most of the Donaldson Line records were lost during the "blitz" in World War II, 1939-1945. This created many problems in the gathering of material for this book on the Company history. For this reason I am very much indebted to the late Mr. Fred A. Donaldson and Mr. Alastair M. Dunnett for their permission to use material in the centenary publication "The Donaldson Line, a Century of Shipping, 1854-1954". The information in Mr. Dunnett's book has been invaluable in my research work.

I would like to thank the World Ship Society members involved with checking the histories and details of the fleet also the provision of additional material. I would especially like to thank Mr. M. Crowdy and Mr. K. O'Donoghue for their support and advice. I would also like to thank the staff and others at the following locations:- The Public Record Office, Kew, Surrey; Lloyds Record and Information Department, London; the Guildhall Library, London; The Historic Photograph Department and the Reading Room at the National Maritime Museum, Greenwich; Research Department, University of Glasgow; Mr. G. Hopner, Dumbarton District Libraries, Dumbarton; Mr. A. Jackson, Strathclyde Regional Archives, Glasgow; Mr. C. Carter, retired editor of "Sea Breezes" for use of material in his magazine; Mr. P. Lasselles, Auckland, New Zealand; Prof. J. Rohwer and publisher Patrick Stephens for use of material in their book "Axis Submarine Successes 1939-1945"; Mr. A. J. Tennant for access to his comprehensive W.W.I. casualty records; Dr. Ricardo Samper, Chargé D'Affaires, Colombian Embassy, London for his efforts in tracking down information on the TRITONIA Memorial project, also Senorita Daisy Barroeta of Venezuela for her accurate translations from Spanish of the considerable amount of information on the TRITONIA; the Scottish Maritime Museum, Irvine; Mr. G. C. Livesey, First Secretary (Commercial) at the British Embassy in Havana, Cuba for his assistance in tracing the final resting place of the last vessel operated by Donaldson Line; Mrs. Clare Sunderland of B. T. Batsford, publishers; Mr. I. Hurley, Assistant Manager, P.R., British Shipbuilders, London; Mr. J. Howard for his photographic assistance; the Library staff at the University of Kent at Canterbury for access to collections; the staff at Grand Manan Museum, N.B., Canada, and students Miss Shari Rayner and Miss Holly Thompson for all the information on the WARWICK and HESTIA; the World Ship Society Photograph Library for use of prints and all other providers of pictures as credited in the text and fleet list; Mr. David Burrell for his time and efforts in collating and providing a considerable quantity of financial and business history on this company and its associates; Mr. Keith Byass for his fine painting of the COLINA in Belle Isle Straits; Mr. Peter Watson of "Design in Cumbria" for giving the cover, maps and diagrams that professional touch; and far from least, my wife, Mary for her almost endless patience and assistance. To any person not included above who assisted one way or another, I extend my gratitude.

Canterbury,   P. J. Telford
Kent,
September, 1989.

DONALDSON LINE OF GLASGOW

In the prosperous years of the mid 19th Century, two sons of a clockmaker, William and John Donaldson, whose ancestors were farmers in Central Scotland, arrived at the bustling port of Glasgow on the River Clyde. In the early days of their employment one worked in a general trader's office and the other with a freight agent. They soon realised the immense potential in the shipping industry. They foresaw the bright future of this expanding port with its international connections exporting machinery and all types of manufactured goods and importing raw materials and foodstuffs from the rest of the world.

John Donaldson
1833-1889

William Falconer Donaldson
1830-1880

While in salaried positions they set out to learn all they could about who and what mattered in the shipping world that surrounded them, their ultimate aim being to become part of the industry. By the mid 1850s they were operating on their own account from premises at No. 62 Buchanan Street, Glasgow, in the heart of the business community.

Their father refused to take any part in the business or in its setting up. Fortunately, their mother and her sister had inherited a family hosiery mill in Anderston, Glasgow, which gave them financial independence. These ladies, with great foresight made the funds available and the Donaldson brothers set out chartering ships and arranging freight for trips to and from the Argentine with calls at ports in Brazil and Uruguay.

This was the beginning of the long, but not unbroken, connections between Scotland and the Argentine. Donaldson's freight from the River Plate in the mid 19th century consisted mainly of hides and bones, destined for the fertiliser industry, and some small shipments of canned and salted meat.

However, as the rail network extended westwards across the vast Pampas, landowners and cattle breeders continually bought up large sections of prime grazing land and were rapidly increasing their herds of beef cattle. The availability of the railway meant that shipments of animals became viable and practicable from the far flung ranches to the ports on the River Plate.

A brief glance into the future, at this point, would show shipments of canned meat being overtaken by frozen meat and then vast quantities of prime chilled beef being taken to European ports. The 1880s saw the Royal Mail Line experimenting with frozen cargoes but many years were to pass before Donaldson Brothers ships ventured into this field.

To return to the latter half of the 1850s we would witness the Donaldson brothers well established. With earnings from their profitable voyages, the two brothers decided that the next step for the "Clyde Line of Packets", as it was known then, would be into direct shipowning. This was to be the foundation of the Donaldson Line of Glasgow. With their reputation in the shipping business, raising the necessary capital was no great problem.

In the Autumn of 1858, A. McMillan & Son, Shipbuilders of Dumbarton, completed the three masted barque JOAN TAYLOR, a vessel of 299 tons, 114 feet in length, with a beam of 25 feet. The master, Captain John Blair, being a shareholder in the vessel, had the pleasure of seeing her named after his niece, Miss Joan Taylor.

On the 20th October, 1858, this sturdy little vessel left Glasgow bound for Liverpool where loading would be completed for the maiden voyage to South America. She arrived in the River Plate 27 days after her departure from Liverpool. Her return to Europe, after a profitable voyage, found the Donaldson brothers busy drawing up contracts with the builders for the construction of another two vessels.

The year 1860 saw the launching of the MARY FALCONER, a ship of 346 tons and named after the brothers' mother. The following year the MARGARET FALCONER was launched. She was a ship of 381 tons named after the mother's sister. The naming of the two vessels paid recognition to the support given by the two ladies in the formation of the business. The local newspaper reported the launch of the first Falconer named ships as follows:-

> "LAUNCH. . On Saturday, Messrs. A. McMillan & Son launched from their building yard a fine clipper barque of 380 tons, the property of Messrs. Donaldson Brothers of Glasgow, and intended for the South American trade.
>
> On leaving the ways the vessel was named, the MARY FALCONER by Miss Donaldson, sister of the enterprising owners. The MARY FALCONER has all the appearances of being a very superior ship, and from her fine water lines is likely to prove an excellent sailer. She is classed A.1 at Lloyds for 10 years and is finished in every respect in the most approved style. Immediately on reaching the water, she was towed up to Glasgow, where she will take in cargo and get ready for sea with all dispatch.
>
> The MARY FALCONER is to be under the experienced command of Captain Pye, and as a fine seagoing vessel will, no doubt, fully sustain the reputation of her builders. The launch was witnessed by a numerous assemblage of ladies and gentlemen from Glasgow, who afterwards adjourned to the drafting loft in connection with the yard, and drank success to the ship, her owners and the builders.
>
> *Dumbarton Herald April 26th 1860*

By the year 1865 the fleet consisted of six vessels. In addition to these ships a number of vessels were on charter and by now the Donaldson Brothers were well established as shipowners. This was the same year that they took delivery of their first composite built ship, this being the URUGUAY whose launch was reported in the Dumbarton Herald as follows:-

> "LAUNCH. . On Tuesday there was a launch from the building yard of Messrs. A. McMillan & Sons, a handsome "Composite" barque of about 500 tons built to class A.1 at Lloyds for 12 years, and intended for Messrs. Donaldson Brothers, Glasgow and South American Line of Packets*. This fine vessel is about 140 feet in length, $26\frac{1}{2}$ feet beam and $16\frac{3}{4}$ feet in depth and has been constructed in the most substantial and complete manner.
>
> The ceremony of naming her was performed by Mrs. John Donaldson, who gave the craft the title of "URUGUAY". After the launch the vessel was taken into the dock to be rigged and fitted out for sea.
>
> Dumbarton Herald April 15th 1865

* not an official title.

The composite method of construction was a timber shell on metal frames, which was replacing all-timber construction. The classification of a vessel was determined by the method of construction, materials used and equipment such as anchors and cables. The timber used for the shell decided the years' life granted on the certificate, the harder the timber the greater the number of years assigned e.g. certain pines gave eight years and teak as many as 14 years. The method of securing the planks to the frames was also taken into account such as galvanised iron bolts replacing wooden dowels and the use of copper fastenings. The underwater area of the hull being protected, from worms and other oceanic "livestock", by felting and yellow metal sheathing. Salting the timber prior to construction added a further year. The classification certificate granted to the URUGUAY contained the following details:- F & Y M., C F., 12 A1. which translates into Felted and Yellow Metal Sheathed. Copper Fastenings used. The '12' indicates twelve years "life" and A1. indicates the top class for insurance purposes.

After the first decade in the business the brothers, who had been watching the development of the marine steam engine, decided that steam was here to stay and that moves must be made in this direction! 1869 saw the start of the construction of the ASTARTE which was launched the following year, 1870, from the yard of Barclay, Curle in Glasgow. The ship was of 1,360 tons, 241 feet in length and had a beam of 32 feet. Her machinery was a 2-cyl. compound steam engine giving 135 H.P. and driving a single screw. As the owners had reservations about the reliability of steam power, the ASTARTE was also brig-rigged to assist in progress and to take over during the predicted mechanical failures.

Early in the 1870s profits were fairly static and little growth was being experienced on the River Plate route. It was therefore decided to open up services to Eastern Canada where trading prospects looked promising and 1874 witnessed the first departure of the ASTARTE on this newly established service. In addition to freight the Donaldson brothers ventured into the carrying of passengers; this also showed much promise. By 1878 regular advertised sailings were operating. Owing to the St. Lawrence River freezing over in winter months, the vessels engaged on this route were switched, in winter, to the South American services which were being maintained by the sailing vessels, CHILIAN, 634 tons and the PERUVIAN, 637 tons.

THE SPLENDID FIRST CLASS FULL POWER SCREW STEAMER

"COLINA,"

A 100 (highest class at Lloyds'), is intended to Sail

FROM GLASGOW

FOR

MONTE VIDEO

AND

BUENOS AYRES,

CALLING AT BORDEAUX, SANTANDER, CORUNA, AND LISBON,

On SATURDAY, the 24th JANUARY,

Receiving Cargo up to Midnight on THURSDAY, the 22nd (unless previously full), but not later.

Bills of Lading, with receipts attached, are required at the Agents' Office, for signature, by Noon on FRIDAY, the 23rd January. Sample Invoices will be received at the Agents' Office up to Twelve o'Clock on the 23rd, and Consignees' despatches will be received up to Twelve o'Clock on the 24th Jan., but not later.

The Steamers of this Line are fitted with every modern improvement, and have accommodation of the very best description for Cabin Passengers; also excellent accommodation for Steerage Passengers. Carries a Surgeon.

FOR RATES OF FREIGHT AND PASSAGE MONEY, AND FOR PLANS OF PASSENGERS' ACCOMMODATION, APPLY TO

DONALDSON BROTHERS,
67 GREAT CLYDE STREET, GLASGOW.

The Owners will not hold themselves bound to take Goods tendered for Shipment which have not been specially agreed for. Receipts for Cargo will only be signed on Forms, which will be supplied by the Agents free of charge. Bills of Lading to be had at the Agents' Office in Glasgow, and no others will be signed.

Each Package to have the Port of Destination marked on it in letters at least two inches long, otherwise the Owners will not be responsible for correct delivery. Freight payable on delivery of Bills of Lading.

COLINA Sailing Card, 1875

Considering the deteriorating political climate in the Argentine against the potential of the strengthening links with Canada, it was decided by the brothers to put the passenger carrying vessels COLINA (I) 2,001 tons and the CYBELE 1,980 tons on the North Atlantic service. These ships could each carry 300 steerage passengers and could accommodate 15 first class passengers in cabins aft. The steerage accommodation was situated midships and in the 'tween decks, an arrangement which reflected the steerage trade. The cabins accommodating the few first class passengers, at the aft end of the vessels, were in a very uncomfortable position on a North Atlantic trader! After a few years, in order to maintain continuity of services, trade was established between Scotland and the Canadian Maritime ports of St. John, New Brunswick and Halifax, Nova Scotia.

Throughout the later 1870s the brothers continued to consolidate their presence on the North Atlantic routes. By now an older brother, Archibald, had joined the firm. When William died in 1880, his two sons joined the now prosperous business and members of the family continued to manage the company efficiently for many years to come.

Other steamers were built for the North Atlantic routes, such as the CONCORDIA (I) 2,152 tons, TITANIA, 2,153 tons and CYNTHIA, 2,152 tons, these vessels being the last iron ships to be built for the Donaldson Brothers. The CONCORDIA had a long career of 28 years during which the only outstanding incident was in July 1896 when she collided with an iceberg off Newfoundland but was able to continue her passage to a safe conclusion.

Passenger services were being maintained, albeit with emigrants, to the promised land of Canada and away from the misery, hunger and unemployment being experienced by many ordinary citizens of Scotland and England. Limited accommodation was available for first class cabin passengers but the emphasis remained with the mass transportation of settlers to the New World with all its opportunities.

Being of farming stock, the Donaldson family were no strangers to cattle and other livestock such as horses. They were now aware of the demand for prime animals in Canada. Their farming expertise along with shipboard and shore facilities made Donaldson Line the main candidate for livestock transportation on the North Atlantic. After much negotiation between Donaldson, the British and the Canadian authorities, the Donaldson Line were declared the best available for the carriage of animals on this tough ocean crossing. The cattle shippers, horse breeders and the attendants travelling with the animals were more than pleased with the conditions and facilities provided by the Donaldson Line on this new service. It was reputed that the Donaldson Line carried animals in conditions far superior to those experienced by emigrants on the Australian services in the 19th century. About the turn of the century the Westbound trade was being matched by the shipments of cattle Eastbound for Scotland, where the port of Glasgow had built facilities to handle shipments of cattle and could accommodate almost 3,000 head at the new lairages at Merklands Wharf.

The routes between Scotland and Canada were not the favourite of seafarers but those who did sail the North Atlantic claimed it was compensated for by the shorter trips. Not for these men the single, long adventure of a voyage, rather a regular shuttle through months of gales and storm force winds and heavy seas, with summer fog and spring ice on the Grand Banks. It is not unknown for fog, gales and ice to come together, nor is it unusual for seafarers, normally trading on fairweather routes, to have been so impressed by the conditions that they have recalled with horror their one and only crossing of the North Atlantic.

One of the major hazards to navigators in the waters around Newfoundland and the Gulf of St. Lawrence is the concentration of icebergs and pack-ice. Sea ice comes in many forms but the iceberg must be considered the most notorious, a reputation enhanced by the "Titanic" incident.

Icebergs in North Atlantic waters originate on the east coast of Greenland where they break away from glaciers. They drift south to Cape Farewell, then north-west to the coast of Baffin Island where the Labrador Current carries them southwards to Newfoundland and into the busy shipping routes across the Grand Banks, a journey which takes between three and four years. Shipping operating between the U.S.A. (and to a lesser extent Canadian maritime ports) and Europe can usually take tracks which avoid most of the iceberg concentrations, but those ships using the Gulf of St. Lawrence and ports in Newfoundland must make their way through areas of ice.

Good visibility, alert look-outs and skilful navigation are needed to get through safely. The use of radar has made the job of the navigator a little easier but it is not infallible since it can fail to detect an iceberg depending on the shape of its surface and the condition of the ice; radar beams may be thrown off into space or virtually absorbed and nothing returns to the ship.

Pack-ice covers the surface of the sea and can be 10 feet thick but in general it is about four feet thick where vessels attempt to steer a path through it. The Gulf of St. Lawrence can have vast areas of pack-ice, and subject to wind directions, it can move around the Gulf so that a vessel which has been steaming along in clear water may find itself trapped by a large mass of ice which has changed direction.

During the late 19th century and the first half of the 20th century shipping did not venture into the St. Lawrence in the winter months, a period from mid-December to mid-April, although some ports in Newfoundland could still be used. When ships started to venture into the Gulf again in April they encountered many hazards with ice and weather.

In the 1880s Donaldsons were fortunate to have secured a contract to carry bulk cargoes of coal from Scotland to the port of Montreal where it was used by the Grand Trunk Railway Company. An early start to the season was beneficial to all but, as the following extract from a Montreal newspaper shows, this brought problems for the ships. The master of CONCORDIA (I) reported:

"The Donaldson Line S.S. CONCORDIA left Glasgow on the 18th April for Montreal. She experienced rough westerly winds all the way across the Atlantic. Fell in with ice on 28th at Cape Ray, found it too heavy to pass through. Ran back as far as St. Pierre Bank to try the Gut.* On the 30th had a heavy gale of easterly wind and fog outside the Gut of Canso. On 1st May passed through the Gut and Northumberland Straits. Saw one field of ice in the Straits of Northumberland which stretched from Cape Egremont to West Point. 2nd May was anchored at the west end of Prince Edward Island during a gale of easterly winds and snow which lasted for 24 hours. 4 a.m. Sunday, left anchorage and proceeded, passed Gaspé at 2.30 p.m. same day, wind North East and snow, which lasted till off Fame Point. From the latter to Father Point had fine, pleasant weather. Received pilot at 1 p.m. and proceeded, reaching Quebec on 5th May at 7.30 p.m. Had to go back to Indian Cove to wait till ice breaks up."

*Gut of Canso. This narrow strip of water between Nova Scotia and Cape Breton Island afforded a sheltered short cut for vessels entering or leaving the Gulf of St. Lawrence from the south. This route has now become restricted due to the construction of a causeway and the provision of a lock does not attract shipping other than local vessels.

"Donaldson" Line.

GLASGOW
TO
QUEBEC AND MONTREAL HALIFAX, N.S. AND BALTIMORE, U.S.
MONTE VIDEO, BUENOS AYRES AND ROSARIO.

Fleet.	*Tons Register.*	*Fleet.*	*Tons Register.*
S.S. AMARYNTHIA, - -	4000	S.S. ALCIDES, - - -	3400
S.S. CONCORDIA, - -	2540	S.S. WARWICK, - - -	2530
S.S. COLINA, - - -	2001	S.S. CIRCE, - - -	2360

GLASGOW
TO
QUEBEC AND MONTREAL.

S.S. ALCIDES, - Friday, 17th April.
S.S. CIRCE, - " 24th
S.S. COLINA, . " 1st May.
S.S. WARWICK. - " 8th
S.S. AMARYNTHIA, " 15th

AND WEEKLY THEREAFTER DURING THE SEASON.

CARGO TAKEN AT THROUGH RATES TO ALL POINTS IN CANADA,
ALSO TO BRITISH COLUMBIA.
ALL QUOTATIONS SUBJECT TO REVISION UNTIL ENGAGEMENT.
THE ABOVE STEAMERS ARE ALL CLASSED 100 A1 AT LLOYD'S, HAVE HIGH POWER,
AND STEAM FAST.

Loading Berth, THE TONGUE, QUEEN'S DOCK.

FOR RATES OF FREIGHT AND PASSAGE, APPLY TO

DONALDSON BROTHERS,
165 St. Vincent Street.

Bills of Lading to be had only at the above address. Receipts for Cargo will only be signed on Forms which will be supplied Free.

GLASGOW, *30th March, 1891*

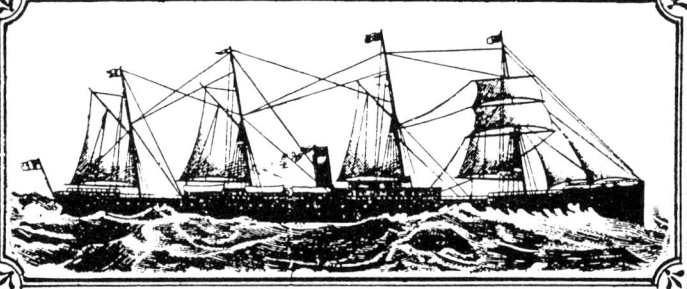

Donaldson Line Sailing Card of 1891

Donaldson Line Sailing Card of 1899

Grand Manan Islands are the final resting places of two Donaldson ships, namely the WARWICK wrecked in December, 1896 and the HESTIA in October, 1909.

When the HESTIA grounded during severe conditions on Old Proprietor Ledges, Grand Manan, 35 lives were lost and the six who survived were very lucky indeed to do so. They clung to the foremast for many hours and then moved to the bridge area but this was soon awash with seas and a rising tide, which can be in excess of 45 feet in this locality. The group, led by the third mate, returned to the foremast where they lashed themselves to anything secure and continued to endure the elements. After approximately 36 hours they were rescued by local fishermen, who landed them at Grand Manan, where they were treated for exposure and other injuries. [See also Appendix 4.]

On a lighter note, a well-known story told within the Company concerned an incident prior to the days of radio being standard equipment in all vessels. It was reported by a lighthouse keeper that an Allan Line vessel had entered the Clyde towing a Donaldson Line vessel. This led to hurriedly arranged meetings between officials of both companies to discuss the salvage claims and compensation for the Allan Line due to their vessel diverting and picking up the Donaldson ship and then towing it back to the Clyde when the Allan Line vessel should have been speeding towards Canada with her passengers and mails. What the lighthouse keeper had actually seen was the Donaldson Line ship skilfully steering the Allan Line vessel from aft thus making for a faster passage to the safety of the Clyde, and, of course a salvage award to Donaldson and the crew of the rescue ship. The Donaldson ship had come across the Allan Line vessel lying helpless, as she had lost her rudder!

In the early 20th century, passenger figures continued to rise on the Canadian service and this in turn involved an increasing number of people returning to Scotland to settle or indulge in well-earned holidays. Thus the company now had two-way traffic and Donaldson Line decided to place orders for three more passenger ships and converted one of the existing ships to increase her passenger carrying capabilities.

Until 1899 all the ships had been owned on the traditional 64 share basis, mainly by the Donaldson family but shares were also held by the shipbuilders, Masters, banks, agents and other parties. It was at the turn of the century that Donaldson Brothers moved to a policy of "single ship" limited liability companies and this policy continued until 1913. Apart from the "Pythia" Steamship Company Limited, all were wound up in September, 1913 when their assets were consolidated into the new Donaldson Line Ltd.

The first company registered was the Glasgow and Newport News Steamship Co. Ltd., formed to own the ALMORA. A major shareholder was the Chesapeake & Ohio Railway Company. The companies that followed reflected the names of the ships and with one exception these companies exhibited a similar pattern. Capital was set at about half the cost of the new ship. Most shares were in Donaldson family hands with small interests held by associates such as Robert Reford Co. Ltd., Donaldson's agent in Montreal, who held some 5% and William Angove their London insurance broker, with 2%. The difference between capital and cost was financed by debenture issues, although in the case of the ATHENIA (I) Vickers, Sons & Maxim Ltd. took £16,000 in shares and £16,000 in debentures.

The exception was the "Pythia" Steamship Company Ltd., formed in 1909 to operate a second-hand vessel taken by Barclay, Curle & Company as a part-payment for a newly built vessel. The capital was all held by Barclay, Curle & Company, until the vessel was sold and the company wound up in 1912.

The following tables illustrate the lifespan and titles of the various Donaldson Line associated companies:-

Company	Incorporated	Liquidated
Glasgow & Newport News S.S. Co. Ltd.	14.11.1899	30.9.1913
Parthenia S.S. Co. Ltd.	14.6.1901	30.9.1913
Athenia S.S. Co. Ltd.	23.4.1904	30.9.1913
Cassandra S.S. Co. Ltd.	22.3.1906	30.9.1913
Pythia S.S. Co. Ltd.	9.12.1909	29.1.1912
Saturnia S.S. Co. Ltd.	26.3.1910	30.9.1913
Letitia S.S. Co. Ltd.	6.3.1912	30.9.1913

At a later date the CORACERO passed through a similar routine but the initial major shareholder was Lithgow, the shipbuilder, prior to Donaldson South American Line Ltd. securing the Lithgow holding in 1924.

Coracero S.S. Co. Ltd.	3.5.1923	16.11.1927

Summary of Management and Parent Company

Company	Incorporated	Renamed†	Liquidated
Donaldson Bros. Ltd.	28.2.1913		13.9.1938
Donaldson Line Ltd.	8.8.1913	20.2.1967	
Donaldson Line Holdings Ltd.		20.2.1967 ↓	1.3.1972
Anchor-Donaldson Ltd.	21.11.1916	10.7.1935	
Donaldson Atlantic Line Ltd.		10.7.1935 ↓	26.5.1954
Donaldson South American Line Ltd.	3.12.1919		21.3.1941
Donaldson Bros. and Black Ltd.	27.6.1938		20.4.1970
Donaldson Line Holdings Ltd.	17.3.1967	24.3.1967 ↓	
Donaldson Line Ltd.		24.3.1967	27.1.1987*

†Dates given in this column are those of the Extraordinary General Meeting at which it was decided to effect the change.

*New company formed in March 1967 as Donaldson Line Holdings Limited; purchased name and goodwill of Donaldson Line Limited for £200,000 and the motor vessel SANTONA (II) for £230,000. Then both companies changed their names. The new company became Donaldson Line Limited which then passed to the Ulster Steamship Co. Ltd., until wound up in 1987.

The old 1913 Donaldson Line Limited became Donaldson Line Holdings Limited, which was wound up in 1972.

To explore deeper into the financial structures over the years of operations of the Donaldson organisation and the Black connection, the reader should refer to Appendix 1.

In 1905 the ATHENIA (I) returned to her builders and conversion work was carried out to increase her passenger accommodation to 50 cabin class and 550 third class passengers. This was followed by the building of the CASSANDRA of 8,135 tons, which could accommodate 200 cabin class of 1,000 third class. She was in turn followed by the SATURNIA and the LETITIA (I), both these vessels being over 8,000 tons.

Dining Area, Steerage Accommodation

SATURNIA Accommodation views, by courtesy of
B. T. Batsford Ltd., London

Second Class Four Berth Cabin

These four ships were popular with thousands of passengers carried across the North Atlantic for many years. They were all triple expansion engined ships with twin screws and capable of 15 knots. With the round trip between Glasgow and Montreal being made in 22 days the four ships could provide a weekly departure from Glasgow and many a sad sight could be seen as relatives lined the docks, and on numerous vantage points along the river banks, to bid farewell to family members who were departing for the new life in Canada and, in many cases, they would never meet again.

1909 was the year that business developed with the Anglo-Newfoundland Development Company, Donaldson Line ships being used to transport newsprint and paper pulp from the newly-opened mills at Botwood, Newfoundland, to the printing presses in London and Manchester.

The Anglo-Newfoundland Development Company had been formed by the Amalgamated Press and Associated Newspapers in an effort to avoid predicted shortages of pulp and newsprint from the United States and Scandinavian sources. The newspaper barons, Lord Northcliffe and Lord Rothermere of the Harmsworth family, undertook the formation of the new company and acquired the land on a 99 year lease. Included in the deal were all the timber and mineral rights of this area of Newfoundland which covered an estimated 4,000 square miles.

By 1905 construction of the mills had started at Grand Falls, N.F., this site being chosen because of its proximity to the Exploits River with its huge waterfalls which provided a source of hydro-electric power for the plant and the expanding township. The site was also on the island railway system and the port of Botwood lay a mere 21 miles along the track to the north east.

Full production commenced in 1909 and by 1912 5,000 tons of paper and pulp were being shipped every three weeks to the United Kingdom. Still the demand for paper could barely be met and this led to the construction of the Imperial Paper Mills at Gravesend on the River Thames. This plant was to become the prime destination for all the pulp shipments from Botwood.

The Anglo-Newfoundland Development Company still flourished together with Grand Falls and its inhabitants in the 1960s when the company was taken over by Price Brothers, the Quebec paper producers, and became part of the Abitibi-Price Company in 1981.

CRANLEY   *National Maritime Museum*

In 1915 when the Anglo-Newfoundland Development Company purchased the CRANLEY through their subsidiary, the Anglo-Newfoundland Steamship Company, Donaldson Brothers managed the vessel and supplied the crews. The CRANLEY was followed by the ALCONDA. In 1916 the Anglo-Newfoundland Development Company took control of the vessels from the

Anglo-Newfoundland Steamship Company although Donaldson continued operating and manning them.

Between the years 1919 and 1938 came the acquisition of the CHALISTER, GERALDINE MARY, ESMOND and finally the ROTHERMERE. The ROTHERMERE and GERALDINE MARY were named after Lord Rothermere and the mother of the two brothers, Geraldine Mary. These two vessels were built for the Anglo-Newfoundland Development Company.

The most widely known name within the history of Donaldson Line must be Anchor-Donaldson Ltd., which operated the Glasgow to East Coast of Canada and United States services with frequent sailings from the Clyde via Liverpool and Belfast. During the 1920s and early 1930s 4,000 to 5,000 passengers passed down the Clyde bound for the Americas each week and Anchor-Donaldson Ltd., carried a large share of these settlers.

Anchor-Donaldson Ltd. was formed in 1916 with a capital base of £250,000 in £1 shares. The holdings were Donaldson Line Ltd., and Donaldson Brothers Ltd., 124,997 shares and Anchor Line (Henderson Bros.) Ltd. 125,000 shares. Since 1911 Anchor Line had been a wholly-owned subsidiary of the Cunard Steam-Ship Co. Ltd., this take-over being seen at the time as a simple means for Cunard to gain entry to the North American routes from the Clyde.

The Donaldson Line ships acquired by Anchor-Donaldson Ltd., together with the goodwill of the service from Glasgow to Eastern Canadian ports, were the ATHENIA (I), SATURNIA, CASSANDRA and the LETITIA (I). The price was £500,000, half being in the form of a 5% mortgage and the balance in shares of £1 value.

Anchor-Donaldson Ltd. ships operated on the parent company routes, the Donaldson ships traded to Canadian ports and the Anchor Line vessels continued to operate to New York and Baltimore. Contrary to popular belief, the ships' staffs were not involved in the arrangements and remained employed directly by their own company with no inter-company movements. The prime aim of Anchor-Donaldson Ltd. was a combined marketing venture for the North American services.

Another shipping company operating from Glasgow to North America and, to a lesser degree, to the ports in the River Plate was the Allan Line which was a well-known and highly respected company, which had been founded in 1807 by a Captain Alex Allan who operated and commanded the brigantine HERO of 175 tons. This vessel was engaged in shipping stores to the Duke of Wellington and his troops, busy fighting the Peninsular War. In 1819 Captain Allan ventured across the Atlantic, in his brigantine JEAN, 169 tons, to Quebec. With his experience on this trip and his confidence in the future of the route to Canada, Captain Allan started building up his fleet of sailing ships.

In 1853 the first steamer was introduced to the Allan Line who, the same year, had just secured the mail contract from the Canadian Government. The Allan Line were to go from strength to strength. They were to experiment with flush decks and with bilge keels, leading to passenger comfort. Soon after the turn of the century they put steam turbines onto the North Atlantic in their new 11,000 ton sister vessels VICTORIAN and VIRGINIAN.

By 1912 the Allan Line Steamship Co. Ltd. were operating 24 ships totalling 200,000 tons. Their ports were Glasgow, Liverpool, London and Plymouth to Canada, United States and the River Plate but changes were near. In 1913, the Donaldson Line took over Allan's South American interests

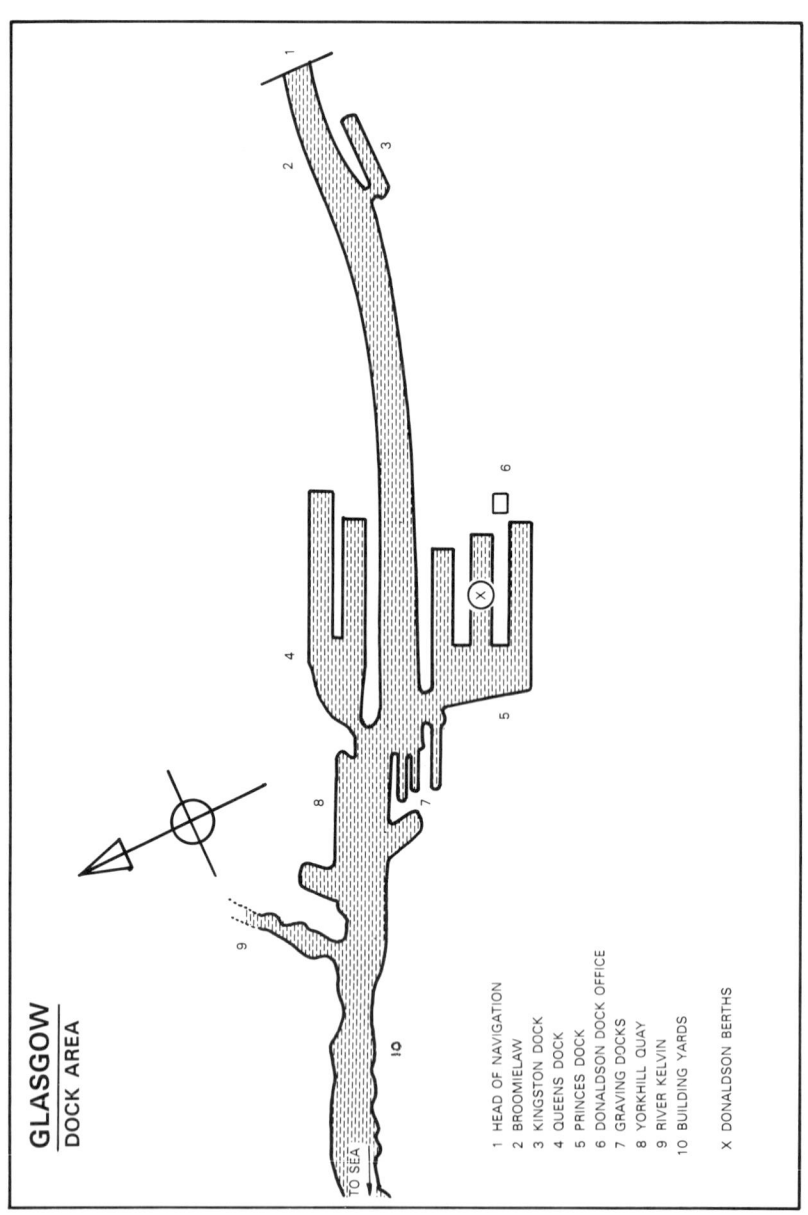

along with the ships on that service. Then in 1915 Allan Line merged with Canadian Pacific thus forming a formidable fleet on the North Atlantic.

The vessels involved in the Donaldson take-over of the Allan Line's River Plate service were the ORCADIAN renamed POLARIA, ONTARIAN renamed CABOTIA and the LIVONIAN. This last named vessel of the three was the oldest and not suitable for Donaldson Line requirements but Allan Line insisted it was part of the deal. The case went to arbitration where Donaldson won; thus this ancient vessel, at the completion of her commitments, passed nominally to Donaldson control but was soon laid up for sale and never operated under the Donaldson Line as a commercial ship. Shortly after this incident the sale of the LIVONIAN for scrap was cancelled and she passed to the Admiralty for eventual use as a block ship at Dover Harbour. [See also Appendix 12.]

The Glasgow Steam Shipping Company Ltd., (J. Black & Co. Ltd., managers) was heavily involved in the deal. They were the Glasgow agents for Allan Line.

With this renewed involvement in the South American route, Donaldson Line, along with the Black connection, hoped to regain a foothold on this service but due to heavy financial commitments in other directions, plans were virtually shelved for a few years and a minor service was maintained with mainly chartered vessels from the Black fleet.

1913 was a major milestone in the history of the Donaldson Line. With heavy investment in ships and services, it was decided by the Board that the Donaldson Line should become a Limited Liability Company and that Donaldson Brothers would become a separate company known as Donaldson Brothers Limited.

At the outbreak of World War I Donaldson Line Ltd. were operating a fleet of 16 ships but were to suffer heavy losses over the next four years, as did the British Merchant Navy as a whole. Of the vessels lost due to enemy action, the sinking of the MARINA (II) in 1916 is believed to be an incident which helped to move President Wilson nearer to involving the United States in the conflict. The MARINA had been carrying American citizens when she was attacked. This created considerable anger with the pro-British citizens in the United States.

WAR EMU on trials *University of Glasgow Archives*

At the termination of hostilities in 1918 the Donaldson Line commenced a programme of tonnage replacement. First came the purchase of the WAR KESTREL 5,214 tons from The Shipping Controller. This vessel was renamed ARGALIA (II), and was closely followed by the acquisition of the WAR VIPER 5,160 tons and WAR EMU 5,244 tons, to be renamed CABOTIA (II) and TRITONIA (III) respectively.

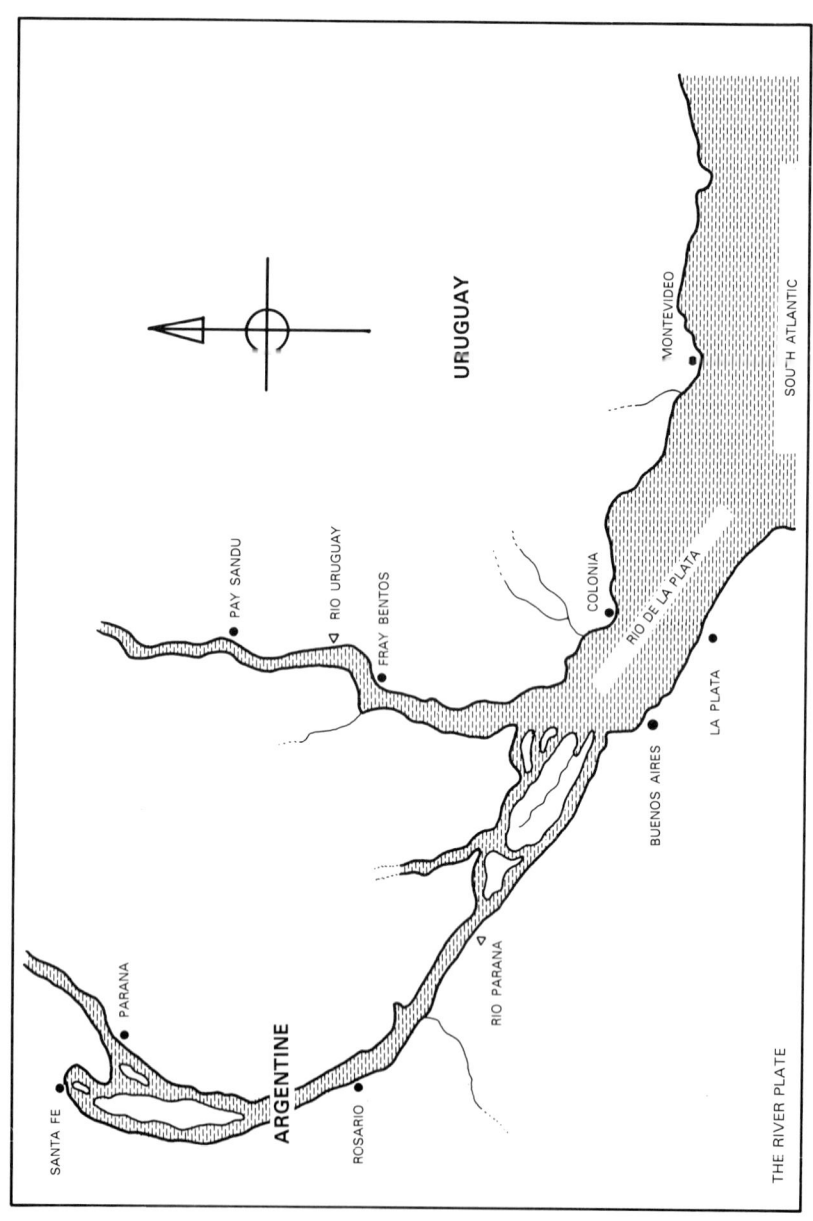

As noted above, ties had been established before the war between Donaldson Line and the Black family-owned Glasgow Steam Shipping Co. Ltd. These resulted from the take-over of the Allan Line's River Plate services and ships and since the take-over Donaldson Line had operated unscheduled services to the Argentine as did the Glasgow Steam Shipping Co. Limited. At times, Donaldson Line chartered vessels owned by Blacks to supplement services on this trade.

Now that the war was over, the time had come to lay plans for expansion and investment in the South American service. Agreement was reached between Donaldson Line Ltd./Glasgow Steam Shipping Co. Ltd./J. Black & Co. and Donaldson Brothers Ltd. to form a new company for the trade, namely the Donaldson South American Line Ltd. This was incorporated 3.12.1919 with an issued capital of £1,000,000. The major shareholdings were:-

Donaldson Line Limited................................509,997
Glasgow S.S. Co. Ltd..................................269,997
Vickers Limited...219,999

The Vickers holding was subsequently purchased by Donaldson Line Limited in 1938.

The company started operations with four ships, with a fifth vessel joining later, in 1923. The D.S.A.L. Ltd. was to be managed by Donaldson Brothers Limited and John Black & Co. Ltd. An important contract was signed with the American owned Armour Meat Packing Company of Chicago for the transportation of chilled and frozen meat from the River Plate to Europe and/or North American ports.

CORDILLERA   *National Maritime Museum*

The new vessels for this service were CORRIENTES (I) 6,863 tons, CORDILLERA 6,865 tons, CORTONA (I) 7,093 tons, CORINALDO (I) 7,131 tons and later the CORACERO 7,252 tons. This last named ship was a product of Lithgows' shipyard in Port Glasgow and was to operate under the "Coracero" Steamship Co. Ltd. Lithgows held 99% of the capital which they sold to Donaldson South American Line Ltd. in 1924. The ship was transferred to D.S.A.L. Ltd. in 1927 and this last of the single ship companies was wound up the same year.

DONALDSON
SOUTH AMERICAN LINE.
REGULAR SERVICE of FAST MAIL STEAMERS
From GLASGOW and LIVERPOOL to MONTE VIDEO & BUENOS AIRES.

	Glasgow	Liverpool
s.s. **CORACERO** ....Sailing	—	.... Jan. 10
s.s. **CORDILLERA** ....Sailing	Jan. 17	.... Jan. 24

Taking Cargo by transhipment to other River Plate Ports

Loading Berths { South Pier, Prince's Dock, Glasgow.
Rail Haulage { West Alexandra Dock, North-Berth, Liverpool.

For Sailings, Rates and other particulars, apply to—
DONALDSON SOUTH AMERICAN LINE, Ltd.
14, St. Vincent Place, GLASGOW.
DONALDSON BROTHERS, Ltd.,
Cunard Building, Water Street, LIVERPOOL, and
16, Gracechurch Street, LONDON, E.C. 3.

A Donaldson South American Line sailing notice of 1925 — *Scottish Maritime Museum*

Further developments took place in 1921 with the acquisition of the Canadian Government services between Canada and the Bristol Channel ports, these ports having easy access to the industrial Midlands. This move marked a significant increase in the limited involvement which the Donaldson Line had hitherto had in the trade to this area.

To improve services to and from eastern Canada, Anchor-Donaldson Ltd. secured a loan early in the 1920s from the Commercial Bank of Scotland Limited of a sum amounting to £400,000. This was used to enable them to take over a vessel, partially built, in the Clyde yard of Fairfield Shipbuilding & Engineering Co. Ltd. This vessel had originated as a Cunard order and was most likely one of a group of six vessels known as the "A" class. Work had been suspended on the vessel after about £300,000 had been spent on her. She was completed in 1925 at a cost of £782,500 and given the name LETITIA (II). A sister ship, from the same yard and completed in 1923, had also been destined for the Cunard fleet but became the Anchor-Donaldson Ltd.'s ATHENIA (II).

Both vessels were to prove very popular with emigrants and regular travellers alike due to the informal atmosphere, fine decor and the continued policy of the Donaldson management to promote comfortable travel for the masses and the discerning traveller alike without ever provision of first class facilities on their vessels. In addition, these ships were noted for their seakeeping abilities. Having twin screws driven by steam turbines they could maintain a service speed in excess of $15\frac{1}{2}$ knots thus providing a fairly fast trip and good timekeeping even in the worst of weather served up by the North Atlantic.

1924/25 marked the inauguration of the three weekly service from Glasgow and Liverpool to the west coast of Canada and the United States, with calls at Los Angeles, San Francisco, Victoria and Vancouver. Other ports were visited given sufficient inducement. New tonnage was provided for this route in the form of the MOVERIA 4,867 tons and the MODAVIA 4,858 tons, both being built byVickers at Barrow in Furness and were the

Donaldson Line's first venture into motor ships. These two vessels were soon to be followed by the GREGALIA 5,802 tons and the SULAIRIA 5,802 tons.

GREGALIA *J. Clarkson*

It was now 70 years since the Donaldson Brothers moved into the world of shipping and throughout they had made notable progress albeit at varying rates, due to political and commercial influences both in the Americas and in Britain. The operation overall had built up a fine reputation and was highly respected by the maritime business world. The ships of the fleet had passed from sail to steam and now, with the completion of the MOVERIA, Donaldson Line were operating their first motor ship.

On the 28th February, 1929, when on passage from Los Angeles to Callao, the TRITONIA (III) called at Buenaventura in Colombia. When working cargo, a fire broke out in the engineroom area and quickly spread towards the holds which, unfortunately, contained large consignments of explosives and inflammable goods. All hands abandoned the vessel and endeavoured to secure assistance from the port authorities in tackling the blaze. Assistance was not obtainable. The chief engineer and the second engineer persuaded the crew of a launch to take them back to the TRITONIA, thinking that just sufficient time was available to flood the ship and put her on the bottom of the harbour thus extinguishing the fire. After opening the required valves the two officers headed for the upper decks but before the launch could take them off the sinking ship, it blew up with devastating effects. Both seamen lost their lives.

Many ships have been lost due to stress of weather in the North Atlantic but companies, like Donaldson Line, who built vessels to withstand the prevailing conditions generally escaped such fates. Unfortunately, there were exceptions, and one was VARDULIA, a ship of 5,691 tons, which was lost with all hands in 1935, when on passage from Hartlepool to Botwood in Newfoundland with a cargo of coal. This vessel was built in 1917 for the Verdun Steamship Co. Ltd. as the VERDUN and bought by Donaldson in 1929. The weather encountered by the VARDULIA was very severe, but not unknown in October. An intense depression was moving N.E. towards the north west coast of Scotland, giving storm conditions ashore as well as at sea. 100 m.p.h. winds were causing much damage around the Clyde area and sending many vessels for shelter. In the VARDULIA's position shelter was not available.

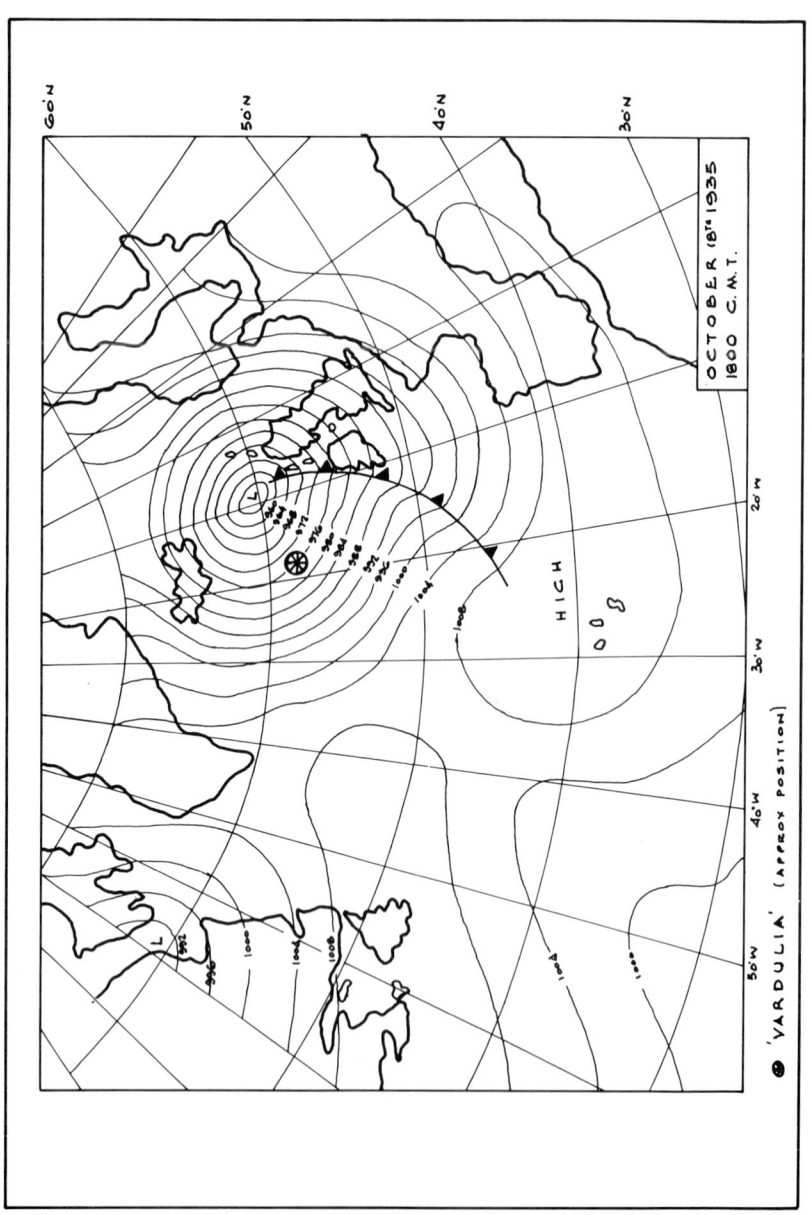

Radio distress signals were received ashore on Friday night the 19th of October; these stated that the crew was abandoning ship by taking to the boats, not an easy task in such conditions. The information received also stated that the vessel had developed a heavy list, due no doubt, to a shift of cargo.

The area was searched by the British ship NEWFOUNDLAND and the Norwegian vessel SONNAVIND but no trace of the VARDULIA or her lifeboats was ever found. The position of the disaster was about 700 miles N.W. of Malin Head, Ireland.

To Masters and Navigators on the North Atlantic, prior to the days of radar equipped ships, fog was classed as the main enemy and it was these conditions which exacted a sad toll on Donaldson ships. Between groundings and collisions eight ships met a premature end to their careers. In the Bay of Fundy area, the world record-breaking tidal flows and currents, added to the weather conditions, could create havoc with the dead reckoning of ships' navigators as they attempted to ascertain a fix, possibly after days without seeing sun or stars, and with fog or heavy snow blocking attempts to pick up landmarks it all added up to make this a rather hostile area for seamen.

In 1934 the Donaldson Line made a major investment by taking over the remains of the Dominion and Leyland Line Ltd. This was an old established family firm which became a public company in 1892 after the death of its founder, Mr. F. R. Leyland. In 1900 Dominion and Leyland bought the West India & Pacific Steamship Company, another old firm which was at that time operating 22 vessels on services to the West Indies, Gulf ports and the west coast of North America.

The principal route was the cotton trade from the Gulf ports to Liverpool and Manchester. The vessels employed on this route were strongly built and of large cubic capacity for their size, and it is stated that they were the largest carriers of cotton from the port of New Orleans.

The take-over by Donaldson Line also involved the Bristol City Line, who received a half-share in the Leyland berthing rights on the routes involved. Donaldson Line obtained four ships: NORWEGIAN 6,366 tons, NUBIAN 6,384 tons, NORTONIAN 6,367 tons, and the DAKOTIAN 6,426 tons; two further vessels passed to the Charente Steamship Co. Ltd., under whose flag they operated for about two years prior to coming under the Donaldson Line. These vessels were the DORELIAN 6,431 tons and the DELILIAN 6,423 tons, and together with the NORWEGIAN they served the Donaldson Line for many years.

During the 1930s the Donaldson Line weathered the economic storms better than many other shipping companies but 1935 witnessed the end of the 19 year old Anchor-Donaldson Ltd., when the Anchor Line passed into liquidation. The Cunard Line voted against the proposed voluntary liquidation of their subsidiary, Anchor Line, which had been running at a loss, but a liquidator was appointed and the assets were bought by the new company, Anchor Line (1935) Limited, which then passed into the control of the Runciman Group. Prior to this event, the Anchor Line deposited a block of shares with the Union Bank in 1932 and another block in 1935 at the same time as 64,286 shares were sold to the Donaldson Line. In view of the majority share holding held by Donaldson the company was renamed Donaldson Atlantic Line Ltd. Later, in 1942, the Union Bank holding was split, part being sold to Donaldson Line and the balance deposited with the Treasury as security for the outstanding guarantee on the LETITIA (II). On completion of the loan repayments, the Treasury holdings passed to the Donaldson Line to make the Donaldson Atlantic Line Limited a fully owned subsidiary.

The Donaldson Atlantic Line Limited continued to operate the ATHENIA (II) and the LETITIA (II) and, bearing in mind the state of trade in the 1930s, Donaldson Atlantic Line Limited did well to turn in profits for the years 1936/38 while other shipping companies had many units of their fleets laid up due to the serious lack of trade around the world.

In 1938 the Donaldson Line Ltd. were operating a total of 11 vessels, namely:-

SALACIA (III)	SULAIRIA	GRACIA (I)
DORELIAN	GREGALIA	PARTHENIA (II)
DELILIAN	MODAVIA	DAKOTIAN
NORWEGIAN	MOVERIA	

The Donaldson Atlantic Line Limited were operating two, LETITIA (II) and ATHENIA (II).

The Donaldson South American Line Limited were operating five:-

CORRIENTES (I)	CORINALDO (I)
CORDILLERA	CORACERO
CORTONA (I)	

In addition, the Anglo-Newfoundland Company vessels under the management of Donaldson were:-

ROTHERMERE	ESMOND	GERALDINE MARY

Thus a total of 21 vessels were under the management of Donaldson Brothers Limited, on services to the west coast of North America, the east coast of Canada and the River Plate. This was a substantial fleet for a family company to operate in such times and they were managing successfully to survive the economic storms although another type of storm cloud was gathering over Europe, in the form of the Nazi German threat which exploded into World War II.

ATHENIA   W.S.S. Brownell collection

The Donaldson Line entry into World War II was very swift and dramatic. On the 3rd of September, 1939, only a mere seven hours after the British Government had declared war with Germany, the ATHENIA (II) was bound for Montreal from Glasgow and Liverpool when she was struck by a torpedo from the German submarine U30 under the command of Ober-leutnant F. J. Lemp. This sinking was in direct contravention of the 1936 Submarine Protocol to the Hague Convention and also against the strict orders of the U-boat fleet High Command's rules on attacks on passenger ships. The falsification of log-books and other record documents, along with the German High Command denying the attack was of their doing, enabled Lemp to manoeuvre his way out of official disciplinary action although behind the scenes he was in serious trouble with his superiors. After the news of the sinking, where 112 lives were lost, many German citizens were less than proud of this attack on an unarmed merchant ship.

The vessels directly involved in the rescue operation were the Norwegian merchant ship KNUTE NELSON, the Swedish yacht SOUTHERN CROSS owned by the arms millionaire Mr. Wenner-Gren and the U.S. Maritime Commission cargo ship CITY OF FLINT. The British destroyers ESCORT, ELECTRA and FAME were also quickly on the scene. By the morning of 4th September, when it was thought the liner had been evacuated, it was discovered that, owing to an oversight, a female patient had been left in the ship's hospital. The Chief Officer with two of the ATHENIA's seamen reboarded the sinking ship and, with the water virtually lapping across the ward deck, they bundled the unconscious patient into a sheet and carried her to the Navy longboat like a sack of laundry.

The ATHENIA sank about 30 minutes after the rescue party reboarded the destroyer with the patient.

There was an ironic sequel to the rescue work and the sinking of the ATHENIA when almost two years later the same Chief Officer was westbound in another Donaldson ship the ESMOND bound for Sydney N.S. from Loch Ewe, Scotland in convoy OB 318. The German submarine U110 under the command of Lemp, now a Kapitan-leutnant, which had been tracking the convoy for some time attacked the ESMOND at midday on the 9th May 1941.

The ESMOND was sunk but all hands were rescued by the escort vessels who commenced a massive depth charge attack on the area and, much to everybody's surprise, U110 surfaced in damaged condition between two British naval vessels. The rescued crew of the ESMOND had a ringside view of the capture of their attacker.

During the assault on the U-boat, by H.M.S. AUBRIETIA, BROADWAY and BULLDOG, the BROADWAY collided with the submarine and lost her port screw as well as being holed. The German crew abandoned ship and were rescued by AUBRIETIA. Meanwhile BULLDOG sent off a longboat to the U-boat and in the next few hours transferred everything possible to the parent warship lying nearby. This booty included tools, papers, instruments, cyphers, radio frequency information and last but not least an Enigma machine which was complete with codes and instructions. This was the first Enigma machine to fall into Allied hands and was put to good use for almost a year, cracking the coded messages to and from the German High Command and the submarine packs. Lemp was lost overboard, presumed drowned, in the action. The submarine sank later, when being towed by one of the destroyers.

One of the most popular cargo vessels within the Donaldson Line fleet was the SALACIA (III). During her 23 years with Donaldson she was deemed to be a "lucky" ship and had excellent sea-keeping qualities with a good turn of speed. This vessel was involved in the North African landings in November 1942 and the following letter reproduced from "The Company

Centenary Book" should be of interest to readers. It is from the Master, Captain A. Bankier to the head office in Glasgow.

"Before I sailed from the Clyde it was disclosed to me that we were on an operational voyage, the purpose of which was the capture of North Africa. In his message to us before sailing Admiral Cunningham called for our best efforts in this operation as it was one of vital importance to the Allied Cause. We left the Clyde on the night of the 22nd October together with another 50 ships forming the slow convoy. The weather was not very promising for the first 24 hours but gradually improved. At the Conference the Commodore, Admiral Troubridge, hoped that, as good weather was of vital importance, those who were in the habit of praying would not forget to remember the weather in their prayers. These prayers must have been answered, for after the first day the weather was favourable right to the end.

The voyage to the Mediterranean was long but uneventful, and we passed Gibraltar in daylight on the 6th November.

SALACIA in war-time   *National Maritime Museum*

The next day the fast transports joined us.

The SALACIA was detailed with four other vessels to take part in the assault in the Bay des Andalouses, about ten miles to the west of Oran. In company with these four ships we parted from the main convoy at 8 p.m. on Saturday, 7th November. We approached our appointed place about midnight where a British submarine was waiting to give our leader the latest information. Just as we stopped the planes carrying the paratroops from Britain were heard passing overhead so we knew everything was going as planned. At 0030 a.m. we stopped about five miles offshore and launched our landing craft. These were then loaded with two mobile guns and two cars each. Thirty men (U.S. Army) went with them and proceeded to the landing beach in company with landing craft from other vessels. It was not an easy job to put 24 ton craft overside in absolute dark with no light then load them. However, everything had been well planned and we had no trouble. The Chief Officer, Mr. C. Porteous**, took charge of this part of the operation and carried it out well.

**Mr. C. Porteous became Master with the Company, his last command being the CAPTAIN COOK on its final two years of operation. In 1960 he was promoted to Assistant Marine Superintendent and became Chief Marine Superintendent for the Company, up to the liquidation in 1967.

After the landing craft had gone in the ships followed in single line into the Bay and anchored as previously arranged about half a mile from the shore. The landing was a complete surprise and no opposition was met until after daylight.

The beach was good, there was no swell, and conditions could not have been better. By daylight nearly 5,000 men had landed at our sector and a considerable number of guns with a supply of ammunition. About 9 a.m. Sunday, 8th November, the mist cleared from the hills and we were seen from the forts above Oran. One of these, Mount Saton, was about eight miles away and stands about 1,000 feet. This fort opened fire on us with 8 inch guns. Two of the ships were hit, but we fortunately escaped, although several shells fell short or just over us. After about an hour and a half of this the Battleship H.M.S. RODNEY hove in sight and to our relief opened fire at once on this particular fort. The first salvo landed squarely on the top guns and they went out of action. We only had a few more shells fired our way, but they fell well clear, and the RODNEY soon demolished the remaining guns which could fire in our direction. A French destroyer had been sent round about 9 a.m. to torpedo the ships in our section but it was met by one of our destroyers H.M.S. BRILLIANT, and we had a grandstand view of the fight. It lasted about 15 minutes, when the French destroyer was sunk. The second destroyer was sunk by H.M.S. AURORA, but we did not see that action.

After this excitement the unloading proceeded in an uneventful way. The operation was hampered at night as we could not use lights, and the evening breeze set up a swell on the beach. For a day or two snipers on the surrounding hills were a bit of a nuisance, but after Oran fell on Tuesday 10th November, all was quiet. The soldiers of the Dock Operating Company who were discharging the ship worked very well, and the U.S. officers and men were very helpful also. We supplied winch drivers when necessary and did everything possible to make the operation a success. The crews of the landing craft deserved great credit as they worked long hours under difficult conditions. The craft were often damaged on the beach, and in some cases were steered by their engines only. All cargo was discharged by 6 p.m. on the 13th November, and our troops and their gear left that night at 10 p.m. SALACIA sailed the following afternoon for Gibraltar arriving there at 9 a.m. on Sunday, 15th November. We left again at 1 a.m. on Tuesday, 17th November, arriving in the Clyde at midnight on the 22nd.

Thus ends the operation known as "Torch No. 1". Before closing this report I must say that all my officers and men in all departments showed great keenness and enthusiasm in carrying out the operation, and all co-operated in the fullest way in making it a success".

This report from the Master of the SALACIA to the Head Office clearly demonstrates the contribution made by all operational merchant vessels and their personnel in times of war. No matter how large or small the incident was or the conditions under which it was carried out, they were treated as a challenge and executed with total professionalism and dedication.

The casualties, 36,000 men in the two wars, reflect this and show the vulnerability of a virtually unarmed force engaged so often in front-line duties.

The LETITIA (II), sistership to the illfated ATHENIA (II), had by contrast a long career and must have been the best known ship that Donaldson Line operated in their years as shipowners.

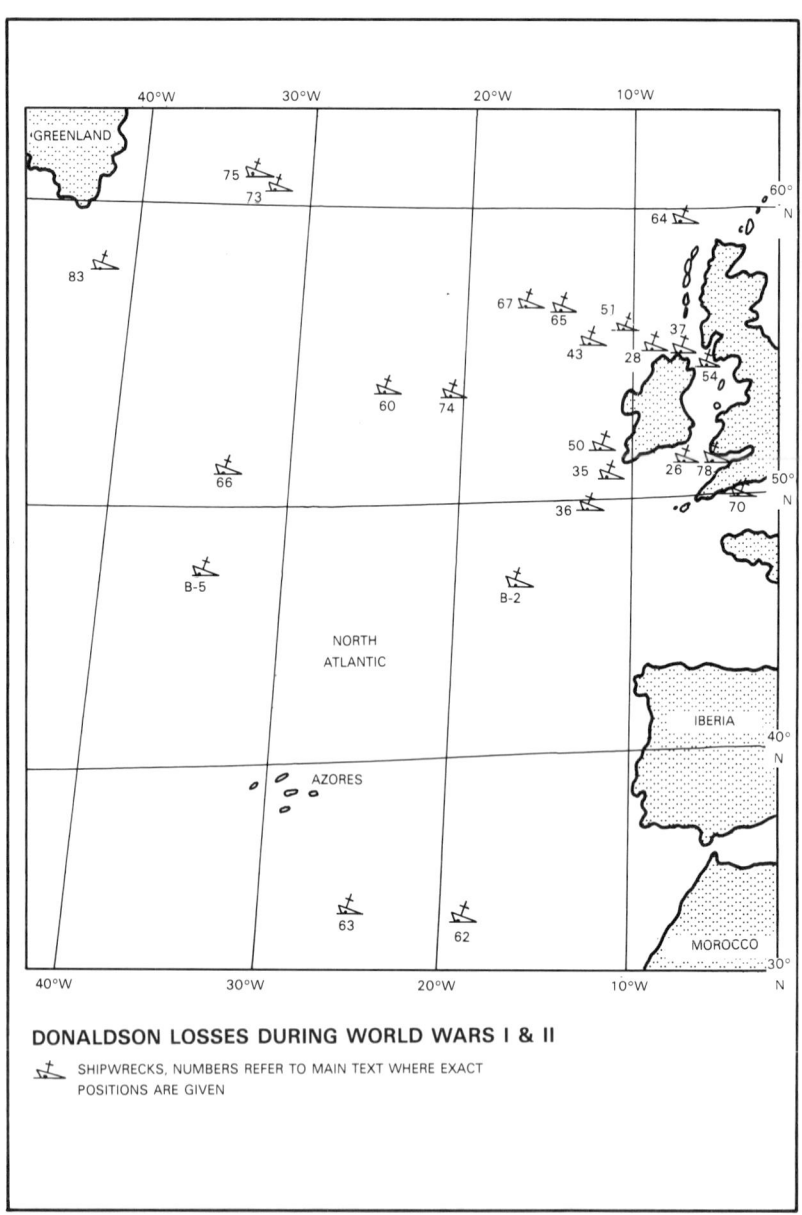

DONALDSON LOSSES DURING WORLD WARS I & II

SHIPWRECKS, NUMBERS REFER TO MAIN TEXT WHERE EXACT POSITIONS ARE GIVEN

When war was declared she was bound down the St. Lawrence from Montreal to Glasgow. On orders from the Admiralty she was turned round and steamed back to Montreal where her passengers were offloaded and she then proceeded to the yard of Canadian Vickers for conversion to an armed merchant cruiser. On completion of the conversion she was assigned

LETITIA following her conversion into a hospital ship   *National Maritime Museum*

to convoy escort duty, mainly in the waters she knew so well, the North Atlantic. Mid-way through the war years she was put on service as a troop transport and saw action at the landings on North Africa, Sicily and Italy. In 1944 she returned to Montreal and Vickers shipyard, where she was converted to a hospital ship for use throughout the world as required. The accommodation was fitted out to cope with a total of 1,000 casualties, with a medical staff of 200 over and above her normal crew. At this time she was reputed to be the finest and best equipped hospital ship afloat.

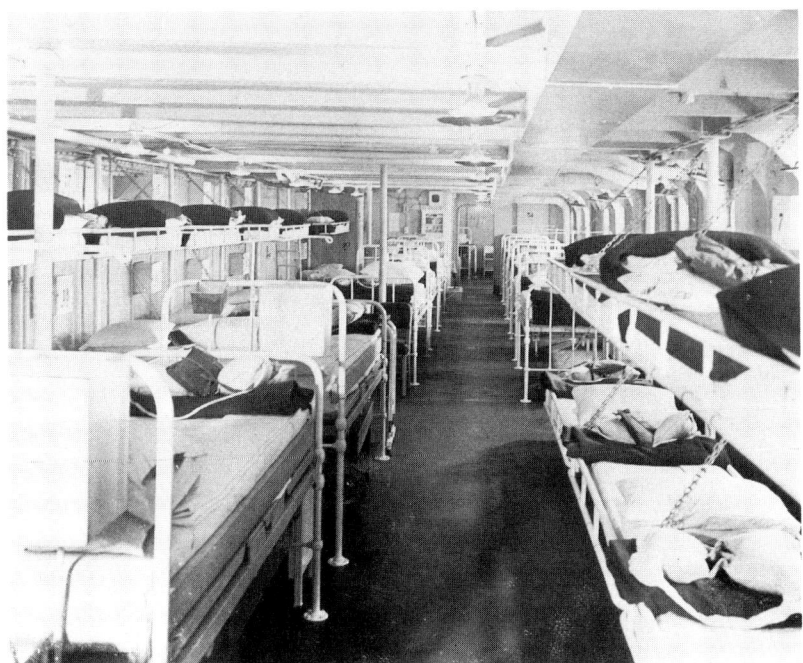

One of the hospital wards aboard **LETITIA**   *Liverpool Daily Post & Echo*

In 1946, after a spell of taking war brides from Britain to Canada, the LETITIA was purchased from the Donaldson Line by the British Government and renamed EMPIRE BRENT. Although she was now state-owned, the running and manning remained with the Donaldson Line. After some trooping duties she was chartered by the Australian Government Immigration Department to carry the £10 immigrants to Sydney. This lasted till 1951 when the charter expired and the British Government then chartered the ship to the New Zealand Government for the U.K.—New Zealand immigration service which was providing free passages to Wellington. Once again the management of the 26 year old ship remained with the Donaldson Line.

For the final phase of her career she was renamed after a well known explorer in the Pacific, CAPTAIN COOK, and by coincidence her first master under this name was Captain James Cook who had been in command of the ATHENIA when she was torpedoed back in 1939.

Initially the New Zealand service was one-way only which entailed the ship returning empty from Wellington to Glasgow, a distance of 11,300 miles. Later she began carrying troops home to the U.K., from places as far apart as Hong Kong, Singapore, Colombo, Aden, Cyprus and Malta. On two separate voyages she brought R.A.F. personnel to Southampton from the atomic bomb testing site at Christmas Island in the Pacific Ocean. To terminate a long and eventful career, stretching over 35 years, the CAPTAIN COOK hauled the Second Battalion New Zealand Regiment from Wellington to Penang and then returned to Lyttleton and Wellington with the 1st Battalion who had completed two years in the Malaysian jungle. On her final return home, after a five month voyage of virtually non-stop steaming, she

CAPTAIN COOK passing Erskine Ferry, 27.2.1960 on her last voyage down the Clyde, bound for the River Fal to be laid up. The Author was her Second Mate when the picture was taken, having served in her for two years, and was subsequently in charge of her while she laid in the Fal.
G. E. Langmuir

laid up in the River Fal, Cornwall for a period of two months. She was purchased in April 1960 by the British Iron & Steel Corporation (Salvage) Ltd. who allocated her to T. W. Ward Ltd., for scrapping at Inverkeithing, Scotland.

In 1946, with the management geared up for expansion after the losses and disruptions of war, the Government ship requisition programme was wound up and vessels were released from control after completing their commitments. The Donaldson South American Line had gone into voluntary liquidation in 1941. 1942, however, had witnessed the formation of the Clyde Stevedoring Company Limited, within the group. The other divisions were the Donaldson Line Limited and the Donaldson Atlantic Line Limited.

TAOS VICTORY as a troopship *A. Holt*

An E.G.M. on the 2nd June 1943 passed a resolution to allow future investment in air transport.

In the early post-war years, the Donaldson Line fleet was reduced to seven vessels, namely, LETITIA (II), CORDILLERA, MOVERIA, DORELIAN, DELILIAN, NORWEGIAN and SALACIA (III). All were over 20 years old except the SALACIA which had been built in 1937.

By 1948 Donaldson had bought seven ships, four American-built and three British. The American vessels were the PARTHENIA (III) ex EMPIRE KANGAROO ex MERCER 6,219 tons, the LISMORIA ex TAOS VICTORY 8,323 tons, LAURENTIA ex MEDINA VICTORY 8,349 tons and the LAKONIA (II) ex SAMTRUSTY 7,227 tons. The two "Victory" ships were fast 17 knot ships driven by steam turbines. After coming into Donaldson ownership and with the cooperation of the Scottish Tourist Board, they were extensively

Troops aboard **TAOS VICTORY**, 28.5.1946 *A. Holt*

converted for the carriage of 55 passengers in a comfortable and informal style, on a regular service between Glasgow and Montreal providing a Glasgow departure every 17 days. Making the crossing in eight days, these two vessels were very popular for many years on this North Atlantic route under the Donaldson Atlantic Line banner. From December through to April, the St. Lawrence river freezes over and is closed to navigation, except for a few specially strengthened vessels. During this time the two Donaldson Line ships operated one round trip each from Glasgow and Liverpool to the west coast of the United States and Canada. This service was always fully booked right up to the time of withdrawal. The ports of call were Los Angeles, San Francisco, Victoria and Vancouver. Other ports were visited if sufficient inducement was on offer.

EMPIRE CROMER passing Bowling, 23.3.1946   *G. E. Langmuir*

In addition to the ex-American tonnage, the following British built "Empire" ships were purchased: CORRIENTES (II) ex EMPIRE CROMER 7,058 tons, GRACIA (II) ex EMPIRE TREASURE 7,040 tons and the CARMIA (II) ex EMPIRE FLAG 7,048 tons. These three vessels were to operate the service from the U.K. to the North Pacific coast throughout the year. After a conversion to the bridge structure, they had accommodation for six passengers and proved to be very popular with people requiring a leisurely trip. The passage from the U.K. to Los Angeles via Curacao and the Panama Canal took about 32 days. The LAKONIA (II) and the PARTHENIA (III) were employed on various services as required but confined to Donaldson routes only.

With hopes that Argentine meat exports would be resumed to the U.K. Donaldsons placed orders for two fully refrigerated ships, which were to be the most advanced chilled meat carriers of the period. The CORTONA (II) 8,289 tons, and driven by steam turbines, was delivered by Hawthorn, Leslie on the Tyne in 1947. She was followed by the motor ship CORINALDO (II) 8,378 tons, built on the Clyde by Charles Connell & Co. Ltd. Both these ships had a good turn of speed and the passage from London to Buenos Aires could be made in under 16 days. They were fitted to carry 12 passengers each and both vessels could take chilled meat in about 50 compartments. The refrigeration machinery was capable of maintaining the temperature in any compartment, even through the hottest tropical conditions encountered on the route, to plus or minus $\frac{1}{4}$ degree Fahrenheit of the shippers' carrying instructions. Chilled meat is a very delicate cargo and has to be treated with considerable respect and vigilance by ships' staff both in the carrying and in the exhaustive preparations in cleaning and maintaining the ship in the condition required by the authorities in the exporting and importing countries. To carry chilled meat at a temperature of 29.5 degrees F. leaves no room for mistakes.

CORTONA in her original livery   W.S.P.L.

The Argentine meat trade, in the early 1950s, did not come up to expectations due to the lack of Government foresight and their lack of ability to reach binding agreements with the Peron regime who were operating extremely tight controls and restrictions on home consumption and exports of meat and meat products. In the summer of 1951 the Argentine Government restricted meat exports to all destinations to 10,000 tons per month, and the British shippers calculated that the U.K. import level would be in the region of 5,000 tons per month. As the Argentine flag ships were receiving preferential treatment, the allocation remaining for the British lines decreased dramatically. Urgent action was needed. The two virtually new and expensive Donaldson Line ships could not lie around idle and therefore were put on charter to companies operating to New Zealand and Australia. After a spell on the Pacific routes they were placed on the U.K./East Coast of Canada services, the CORINALDO mainly operating from Glasgow while the CORTONA was based on the Bristol Channel ports.

In the early and middle 1950s the westbound cargo availability on the Canadian service was very poor and the eastbound freight was of low grade, thus earnings were low and too many ships were chasing too few cargoes. The picture looked grim. However, 1955 witnessed the end of the Peron regime in the Argentine due to a Military take-over of the country. This led to the doors of the lucrative meat trade being cracked open again.

The CORTONA was taken off the North Atlantic and her insulation was refitted. She departed South for the River Plate in May 1955 to resume the trade she had been built for nearly eight years previously. The CORINALDO

BUENOS AIRES
SOUTH DOCK AREA

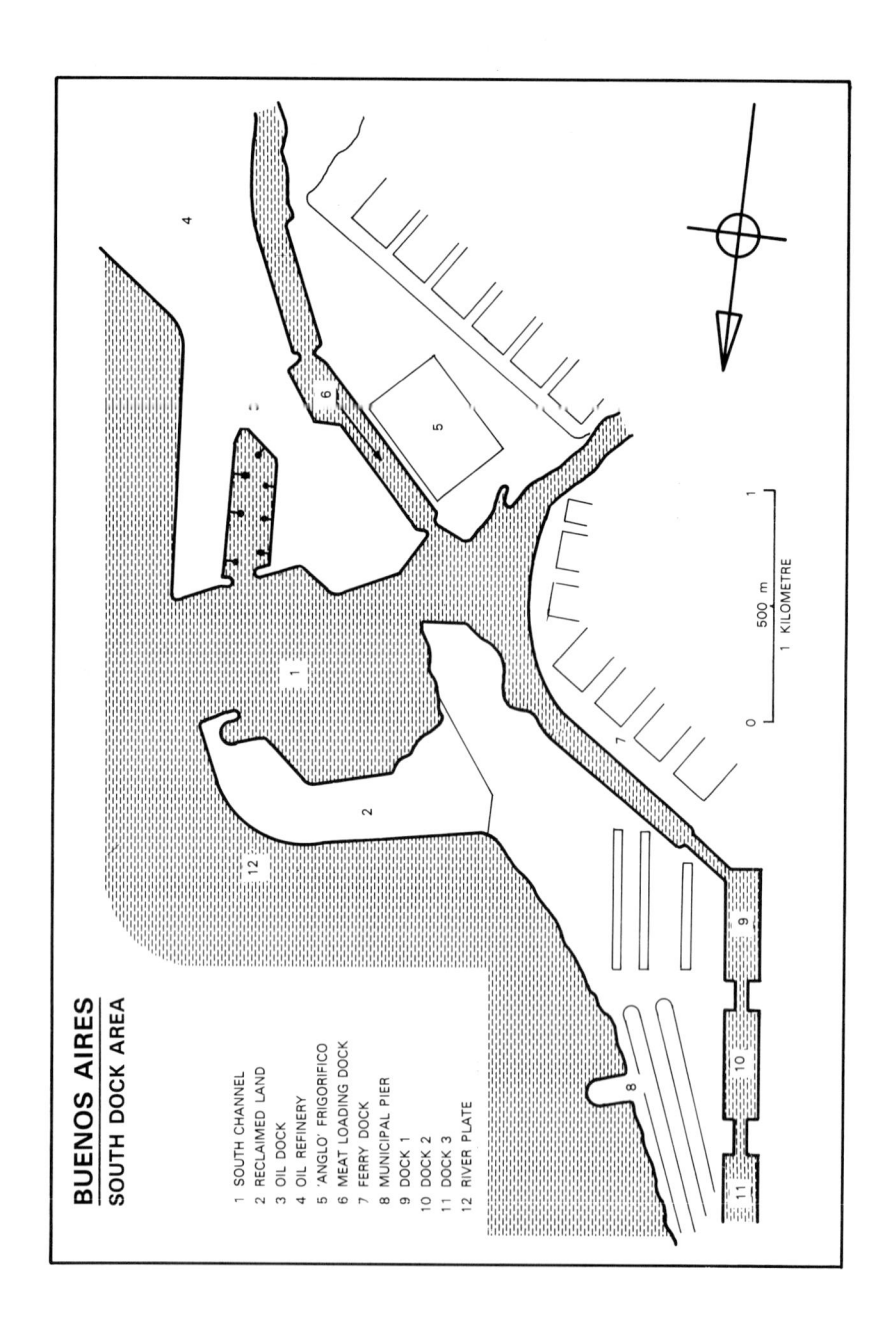

1 SOUTH CHANNEL
2 RECLAIMED LAND
3 OIL DOCK
4 OIL REFINERY
5 'ANGLO' FRIGORIFICO
6 MEAT LOADING DOCK
7 FERRY DOCK
8 MUNICIPAL PIER
9 DOCK 1
10 DOCK 2
11 DOCK 3
12 RIVER PLATE

followed her sister two years later. It was now virtually 100 years since the route was started by William and John Donaldson with the little sailing vessel JOAN TAYLOR. Alas! The commercial climate in 1958 was considerably different from 1858 and operating a shipping company was of greater complexity and more uncertainty than in the days when profit margins were much greater, and taxation less complex, thus allowing more confidence for the ship owner to invest in new tonnage and ventures to other parts of the globe.

In 1954 the Donaldson Atlantic Line Ltd. was wound up and the vessels came directly under the parent company, the Donaldson Line Ltd. (Donaldson Bros. & Black Ltd., managers). This period also witnessed the end of the North Pacific Coast services and the vessels on this route were withdrawn. The three ships involved passed to the Blue Star Line, namely, GRACIA (II), CARMIA (II) and CORRIENTES (II). The third of the trio did not remain for long with Blue Star Line and a proposed name change did not occur. She was resold to Hong Kong buyers.

CORINALDO *Alex Duncan*

The remaining British operators on this route with Blue Star Line were Furness, Withy and Royal Mail Lines with the Johnson Line of Sweden providing tough competition with their modern fleet of 20 knot vessels.

When the CORTONA was taken off the North Atlantic and transferred to the River Plate service, the Donaldson Line purchased the CHARLTON PRIDE from the Charlton Steam Shipping Co. Ltd. This was a vessel of 8,418 tons built in 1941 as the troop-ship EMPIRE PRIDE. Under that name she carried up to 2,200 troops a voyage during the war years and was involved in the landings at Madagascar in 1942 as well as North Africa, Sicily and the South of France. From the end of hostilities until 1954 she continued to operate as a troop transport with a limitation of 1,600 to comply with regulations in force at that time.

The Ministry of Transport sold her in 1954 to Charlton Steam Shipping Co. Ltd. and, after her conversion to a cargo vessel at Lubeck, she operated as the CHARLTON PRIDE until Donaldson bought her. She was overhauled at Rotterdam and took up service on the North Atlantic for Donaldson as the CALGARIA. She could carry 12 passengers in accommodation fitted to a very high standard with modern decor. Facilities for approximately 800 head of livestock were provided in the shelter deck which included sufficient space to stow food and bedding for a passage of up to nine or ten days. Fresh water was laid on to the stock areas and the stalls were portable to allow general cargo stowage space on the eastbound passage. The large raised poop deck of this vessel was fitted with stalls to enable about 36 head of cattle to be accommodated. The usual occupants of this deck were Polled Herefords bound for the British breeders from the mid-west of Canada.

She was a powerful, well built ship but had, from the time of building, been fitted with the old type screws which had the blades bolted onto the boss and these gave a very high "slip". Donaldsons, acting on advice of naval architects, had manganese bronze propellers cast and fitted. These proved to be a good investment and the slip dropped considerably with the speed going up to 18 knots from around 14 knots.

During 1957, the Donaldson Line moved into a new venture. With small chartered vessels they launched a new service to the Great Lakes with calls at Toronto, Hamilton, Sarnia and Windsor. The outlook seemed promising and led to Donaldson Line placing an order for a ship of about 5,000 tons, with Hall, Russell & Co. Ltd., Aberdeen. This vessel was to be constructed to meet the St. Lawrence Seaway and Welland Canal Regulations. Sadly this order was cancelled and replaced with a contract to build two smaller ships of about 1,600 tons. This, in the view of the sea-going staff, was a mistake. These vessels would be suitable for trade within the Lakes and the Gulf of St. Lawrence but it was felt too small and low powered for regular North Atlantic trading and the carrying capabilities were also too limited. This opinion proved to be correct in the longer term as both ships were lengthened by the insertion of an additional hold, six years after construction.

The St. Lawrence Seaway opened in 1959 and the first of the new ships, the SANTONA (II) 1,769 tons started off the service. She was to be followed by her sistership COLINA (II) 1,776 tons, in 1960. Engines and accommodation were situated aft, thus the officers and ratings were in very much the same unfortunate position as the first class passengers had been in the old ASTARTE almost 100 years before. During the winter months both vessels operated in the Mediterranean under charter to companies such as the Zim Line of Israel, Ellerman Lines of Liverpool and Johnston Warren also of Liverpool. Both ships proved to be very suitable for this trade.

LETITIA *W.S.P.L.*

1961 saw the delivery of LETITIA (III), a motor vessel of 4,667 tons. This ship was to be the last to be built for the long-established company.

With the arrival of containerisation of freight and purpose built vessels to carry them, the decline in passenger traffic, increasing crew and maintenance costs — especially bearing in mind the labour intensive docks with their outdated methods and handling systems resulting in long periods in port — the signs for the future were rather ominous.

As noted earlier, 1943 was the year the Board passed a resolution allowing for future investment in air travel. Twenty years later this would come to pass. In 1963 the Chairman of Caledonian Airways (Prestwick) Ltd., a Mr. Adam Thompson, approached the Donaldson Line with an urgent request for financial assistance in meeting outstanding fuel bills. This request was agreed to but the Donaldson Line board believed this could be the time for diversification and, in the wake of intensive meetings, they not only cleared the fuel bills but invested a capital sum of £200,000 and in addition to this sum bought up 25% of the shares in Caledonian Airways. The White Heather Travel Agency in Glasgow was also taken over, all with the aim of selling charter flights to the Mediterranean and Near East destinations. Many of the route applications were objected to by established operators such as British Overseas Airways Corporation and other, short haul, carriers. The objections were upheld by the Civil Aviation Licensing Board and trips such as pilgrimages to Israel and holiday flights to Spain were blocked. The main traffic was restricted to Trans-Atlantic operations.

The disposal of the fleet had now started. The war-time built LAKONIA was sold in 1962 and the CALGARIA in 1963. No replacement tonnage was on order. Business struggled along to 1966 when further important decisions had to be made. This was the year that passenger services were to end and the two vessels involved, LISMORIA and LAURENTIA, thereafter operated as freight ships on the North Atlantic trade.

LISMORIA in Princes Dock, Glasgow, 6.4.1957   *W.S.S. Wylie collection*

Mr Fred Donaldson, Chairman, in his address to shareholders in March made the following observations:-

1. The Company was experiencing severe reductions in earnings on the River Plate service due to operational costs such as the latest pay award to seafarers.
2. Shortage of labour in some ports led to high overtime payments being paid to dock staff in an attempt to maintain the departure schedules.
3. Domestic demand for meat in the Argentine could not be met by local suppliers therefore exports suffered drastically in the chilled and frozen sector of the market.
4. Canadian trade was improving but was offset by heavy overheads.
5. Great Lakes trade static.
6. Bristol Channel trade poor throughout the season.
7. Air and travel services showing promise.

The shipping industry was about to experience the most radical change since power ousted sail, and shipowners along with their staffs were to suffer considerable upheaval undreamed of a few short years before. This was the dawn of containerisation which added up to much larger ships, smaller crews, faster passages, quicker turn-round in port and last but not least colossal investment in new tonnage, containers and all the shore facilities to meet the demand. For a small company such as the Donaldson Line Ltd. to compete in this field was impossible. Even to join forces with a larger operator was out of the question due to the tremendous amount of capital required. It was clearly the time to wind up the business and this was done at the beginning of 1967 by calling in the receiver to put the Company into voluntary liquidation.

The fleet was disposed of as follows:- LAURENTIA and LISMORIA were sold for scrap. The CORTONA and CORINALDO went to Greek interests, the CORINALDO passed briefly to China Navigation Co., prior to going under the Liberian flag. The COLINA was sold to a Canadian company based in St. Johns, Newfoundland, also for further trading. The LETITIA was taken over by a leasing company and placed under the management of another old Glasgow firm, J. & J. Denholm. The SANTONA was dealt with under different arrangements.

SANTONA inward-bound passing Port Glasgow, 7.7.1962   *W.S.S. Wylie collection*

A new company was formed in March 1967, Donaldson Line Holdings Limited, which purchased the name and the goodwill of the Donaldson Line Ltd. for £200,000 and the SANTONA for £230,000. Then Donaldson Line Holdings Ltd. changed its name to the Donaldson Line Ltd., and passed to the ownership of The Ulster Steamship Co. Ltd.

The old Donaldson Line became Donaldson Line Holdings Ltd. and continued to operate in various spheres until liquidated in 1972.

Its 10% share of the River Plate meat trade was passed over to Blue Star Line, the largest of the remaining British operators on this route, the others being Royal Mail Lines and Houlder Brothers.

Donaldson Line Holdings Ltd. continued in business with the share in Caledonian Airways (Prestwick) Ltd., but this was sold to Lyle Shipping Company Ltd., along with the Travel Agency, in 1968.

Finally in 1972 The Clyde Port Authority took over the remaining assets of the old company, the Clyde Stevedoring Company Limited.

The Receiver called in to wind up the Company in 1967 was:
W. A. Brown C.A.
112 West George Street
Glasgow C.2
Scotland

At a Board meeting on the 23rd of May 1967 a resolution was passed placing the Company in voluntary liquidation. The shareholders were paid as follows:

Preference shares of £1 were repaid at 22/6 per share on the 30th June 1967. Holders of the Ordinary shares of £1 and the "A" Ordinary shares received the following distributions:-

```
30th June 1967........................27/6
29th September 1967................ 11/0
            TOTAL          38/6
```

Prior to the Liquidation announcements, shares in the Donaldson Line were trading around the 18/- level but with assets being realised at considerably more than the Board's conservative estimates along with 11th hour speculators coming on the scene, the shareholders did rather well out of the winding up and at the Chairman's suggestion they contributed towards a fund to aid long-serving members of the staff who would now be without employment. This fund was generously contributed to and the subsequent payments helped to alleviate hardships met by the recipients.

Fred Alistair Donaldson
1909-1988

The Donaldson Line Board in this final year of trading as ship-owners consisted of the following directors:

F. A. Donaldson . . . Chairman

I. H. S. Black
R. G. L. McCallum
A. N. Donaldson
P. G. Donaldson
D. L. Richardson
W. A. White
W. Logan
D. S. Black

1967 commenced with a fleet of seven vessels with a combined tonnage of more than 41,000 tons and ended with none.

This sad end to an old and respected shipping company was regretted by all within the shipping world. Many of the staff both ashore and afloat had spent all their working lives with the firm. Since the liquidation of the Donaldson Line Ltd., many reputable British shipping concerns have gone out of business or moved to foreign flags. The experience endured by the Donaldson Line and its staff in the mid 1960s can, with hindsight, be seen as the beginning of the decline of the British Merchant Service.

FLEET LIST NOTES

The notation '(I)', '(II)' etc. after a ship's name indicates that she is the first, second, etc., ship of that name in the fleet. The dates following the name are those of entering and leaving the fleet, or coming under and leaving the management of the company. The histories are in chronological order according to date of completion or acquisition.

On the first line is given the ship's Official Number (ON) in the British Registry, followed by her tonnages gross ('g') and net ('n'). Dimensions given are the registered length x beam x depth in feet and tenths for ships numbered 1-88, and all managed ships, and for ships 89-96 the overall length x beam x draught in feet and inches. These details are as recorded in "Lloyd's Register".

On the second line are given details of the machinery ('cyl.' prefixed by a number indicates the number of cylinders in the engine) and the recorded horse power of the engine. 'N.H.P.' is Nominal Horse Power, 'I.H.P.' is Indicated Horse Power and 'S.H.P.' is Shaft Horse Power.

FLEET LIST: OWNED SHIPS
AND THOSE OF ANGLO-NEWFOUNDLAND DEVELOPMENT COMPANY

JOAN TAYLOR *From an oil painting*

1. **JOAN TAYLOR (1858-1864)** Wooden barque.
ON. 22088. 299g, 299n. 114.4 × 25.1 × 16.0 feet.
Classification life: 10 years.
21.9.1858: Launched by A. McMillan & Son, Dumbarton (Yard No. 87) for Donaldson Brothers. *8.1864:* Sold to G. T. Lawrence, Hull. *24.4.1866:* Foundered off S.W. Ireland when on passage from Liverpool to Barbados.

2. **MARY FALCONER (1860-1871)** Wooden barque.
ON. 28486. 346g, 346n. 120.5 × 26.4 × 16.6 feet.
Classification life: 10 years.
24.4.1860: Launched by A. McMillan & Son, Dumbarton (Yard No. 95) for Donaldson Brothers. *4.1871:* Sold to A. McKinnon, Greenock. *8.1873:* Sold to Dixon & Co. London. *1876:* Sold to R. Ryley, London and later in *1876* reverted to Dixon & Co. London. *1877:* Sold to Belgian owners. *1879:* Sold to Belgian shipbreakers for demolition.

3. **MARGARET FALCONER (1861-1868)** Wooden barque.
ON. 43689. 381g, 381n. 127.5 × 26.5 × 16.7 feet.
Classification life: 10 years.
18.9.1861: Launched by A. McMillan & Son, Dumbarton (Yard No. 102) for Donaldson Brothers. *10.1868:* Sold to I. Jackson, London. *1877:* Sold to Stephenson & Jackson, London. *1882:* Sold to Craandyk & Dudok de Wit, Holland, and renamed SLANGEVECHT. *7.1885:* Sustained damage during a voyage from Colombo to New York and put into Port Louis, Mauritius. *1886:* Condemned and sold for scrapping.

4. **LA PLATA (1863-1872)** Wooden barque.
ON. 45961. 393g, 393n. 130.0 × 26.5 × 16.7 feet.
Classification life: 10 years.
4.4.1863: Launched by A. McMillan & Son, Dumbarton (Yard No. 111) for Donaldson Brothers. *1872:* Sold to A. Cross and W. Kennedy, Chile. *1875:* Sold to F. Peed, Chile. *1882:* Scrapped in Chile.

5. PARANA (1863-1875) Wooden barque.
ON. 47824. 399g, 399n. 129.7 × 26.9 × 16.8 feet.
Classification life: 10 years.
20.10.1863: Launched by A. McMillan & Son, Dumbarton (Yard No. 114) for Donaldson Brothers. *2.1875:* Sold to A. McKinnon, Glasgow. *12.1878:* Sold to H. Mentz, Germany. *1883:* Sold to E. Burchard, Germany. *31.3.1897:* Abandoned in the North Sea, west of Hanstholm, Denmark, when on passage from Sunderland to Danzig, with a cargo of coal.

6. URUGUAY (1865-1866) Composite barque.
ON. 50539. 476g, 476n. 143.0 × 27.1 × 16.5 feet.
Classification life: 12 years.
11.4.1865: Launched by A. McMillan & Son, Dumbarton (Yard No. 121) for Donaldson Brothers. *12.1866:* Foundered while on passage from Valparaiso to Liverpool on her second voyage. 13 of her crew were lost.

7. COLORADO (1865-1887) Composite barque.
ON. 52625. 544g, 526n. 152.8 × 28.1 × 17.5 feet.
Classification life: 12 years.
8.1865: Launched by A. McMillan & Son, Dumbarton (Yard No. 122) for Donaldson Brothers. *5.7.1887:* Wrecked on Cape St Vincent, Tierra del Fuego, Argentina while on passage from Hull to Valparaiso with coal. Seven members of her crew were lost.

8. MIAMI (1867-1877) Iron barque.
ON. 58320. 498g, 498n. 154.0 × 27.7 × 17.3 feet.
20.6.1867: Launched by Dobie & Company, Glasgow (Yard No. 24) for Donaldson Brothers. *29.11.1877:* Wrecked at Molle Bay, Peru, while on passage from Iquique to Molle with a cargo of nitrate of soda.

9. IMUNCINA (1867-1889) Iron barque.
ON. 60326. 583g, 583n. 165.6 × 30.2 × 17.4 feet.
20.10.1867: Launched by Dobie & Company, Glasgow (Yard No. 27) for Donaldson Brothers. *2.7.1889:* Badly damaged by fire while loading at Pisagua, Chile and abandoned to the insurance underwriters. Cargo being handled, nitrate of soda. *1890:* Sold by the underwriters to D. Schiattino (later D. Schiattino & Perfetti), Chile and renamed REINA MARGARITA. *1899:* Sold to Filippo Schiaffino fu Prospero, Italy and renamed REGINA. *1904:* Sold to A. Gotusso, Italy. *9.12.1907:* Wrecked at Portsall whilst on a voyage from Fowey to Genoa with a cargo of china clay.

MARANON *From an oil painting*

10. MARANON (1868-1874) Iron barque.
ON. 60376. 605g, 585n. 170.6 × 30.4 × 17.4 feet.
17.8.1868: Launched by Dobie & Co., Glasgow (Yard No. 32) for Donaldson Brothers. *23.12.1874:* Destroyed by fire when loading nitrate of soda at Antofagasta, Chile, with the loss of one life. *1875:* Hulk bought by J. Thomas Worth, the "Nitrate King", who operated her as a water barge until she was lost, in *1879,* during the war between Peru and Chile.

SANTONA *From an oil painting*

11. SANTONA (I) (1869-1891) Iron ship, later a barque.
ON. 60447. 896g, 855n. 203.4 × 32.1 × 19.3 feet.
7.8.1869: Launched by Dobie & Company, Glasgow (Yard No. 41) for Donaldson Brothers. *1879:* Refitted and rerigged as a barque. *3.10.1891:* Wrecked at Palmillas Point, Matanzas, Chile when on passage from Coquimbo to Matanzas in ballast. The entire crew was lost.

Builders' rigging plan of **ASTARTE** *Company Archives*

12. ASTARTE (1870-1878) Iron steamship, brig-rigged.
ON. 63786. 1,360g, 863n. 241.1 × 32.4 × 23.7 feet.
Compound inverted direct acting 2-cyl. steam engine of 135 N.H.P. made by the shipbuilder.
Accommodation provided for steerage and a few first class passengers.
16.8.1870: Launched by Barclay, Curle & Co., Glasgow (Yard No. 204) for Donaldson Brothers. *10.1870:* Completed. *31.1.1878:* Wrecked off Cape St. Mary, Uruguay, with the loss of 30 lives, when on passage from Cardiff to Montevideo.

MARINA   *From an oil painting*

13. **MARINA (I) (1870-1873)** Iron steamship, initially brig-rigged.
ON. 63800. 1,358g, 861n. 240.8 × 32.6 × 23.8 feet.
Compound inverted direct acting 2-cyl. steam engine of 135 N.H.P. made by the shipbuilder.
Fitted with passenger accommodation.
25.10.1870: Launched by Barclay, Curle & Co., Glasgow (Yard No. 205) for Donaldson Bros. *12.1870:* Completed. *7.1873:* Sold to The Brazil Steam Ship Co. Ltd., Liverpool. *1877:* Sold to Robert Alexander, later Alexander & Radcliffe and subsequently Robert Alexander & Co., Liverpool. *1882:* Sold to Rocco Piaggo e Figli, Italy and renamed MARIA. *7.1885:* Sold to Navigazione Generale Italiana, Italy and renamed PARAGUAY. *1890:* Fitted with new boilers and machinery converted to triple expansion by Continental Lead and Iron Co., Ltd. *1910:* Sold to S.A. Nazionale di Servizi Marittimi, Italy. *1913:* Sold to G. Randazzo, Italy, and renamed TORERO. *1928:* Sold to Ang. Berterello, and broken up in Italy.

14. **COLINA (I) (1872-1895)** Iron steamship, initially brig-rigged.
ON. 68022. 2,001g, 1,297n. 319.3 × 34.8 × 25.6 feet.
Compound inverted 2-cyl. steam engine of 265 N.H.P. made by the shipbuilder.
Fitted with passenger accommodation.
31.10.1872: Launched by Barclay, Curle & Co., Glasgow (Yard No. 229) for Donaldson Brothers. *2.1873:* Completed. *1883:* Reboilered. *9.1895:* Sold to Edward Watson, Glasgow. *3.1898:* Sold to G. Bagnasco, Italy. *4.1898:* Scrapped at Genoa.

15. **CYBELE (1874-1880)** Iron steamship, brig-rigged.
ON. 68078. 1,980g, 1,278n. 319.6 × 34.6 × 25.5 feet.
Compound inverted 2-cyl. steam engine of 300 N.H.P. made by the shipbuilder.
Fitted with passenger accommodation.
21.1.1874: Launched by Alexander Stephen and Sons, Glasgow (Yard No. 168) for Donaldson Brothers. *3.1874:* Completed. *13.8.1880:* Wrecked at Heath Point, Anticosti Island, Gulf of St. Lawrence, while on passage from Glasgow to Montreal with passengers and general cargo.

16. **CHILIAN (1875-1892)** Iron barque.
ON. 73791. 634g, 601n. 176.7 × 30.1 × 17.4 feet.
29.9.1875: Launched by D. & W. Henderson & Co., Glasgow (Yard No. 166) for Donaldson Brothers. *15.5.1892:* Wrecked on Serpent Bank, San Blas Bay, Patagones, Argentina while on passage from Cardiff to Iquique with a cargo of patent fuel.

PERUVIAN, wrecked at Seaford — *National Maritime Museum*

17. PERUVIAN (1875-1890) Iron barque.
ON. 73807. 637g, 608n. 176.5 × 30.1 × 17.4 feet.
30.11.1875: Launched by D. & W. Henderson & Co., Glasgow (Yard No. 167) for Donaldson Brothers. *8.1890:* Sold to A/S Peruvian (L. A. Mathiasen, manager), Denmark. *8.2.1899:* Wrecked near Seaford, Sussex, while on passage from Esmeraldes, Equador, to Hamburg, with a cargo of ivory nuts and logs.

18. EIRENE (1878-1879) Iron steamship, brig-rigged.
ON. 78592. 2,035g, 1,317n. 321.0 × 35.4 × 25.1 feet.
Compound inverted direct acting 2-cyl. steam engine of 382 N.H.P. made by the shipbuilder.
Fitted with passenger accommodation.
22.2.1878: Launched by D. & W. Henderson & Co., Glasgow (Yard No. 182) for Donaldson Brothers. *4.1878:* Completed. *30.9.1879:* Wrecked on Seal Rocks, Strait of Belle Isle, Labrador, while on passage from Montreal to Glasgow with a cargo of grain and flour. Nine passengers were on board.

19. CYNTHIA (1880-1889) Iron steamship.
ON. 82317. 2,152g, 1,410n. 329.7 × 36.8 × 25.1 feet.
Compound inverted 2-cyl. steam engine of 460 N.H.P. made by the shipbuilder.
Fitted with passenger accommodation.
26.5.1880: Launched by D. & W. Henderson & Co., Glasgow (Yard No. 210) for Donaldson Brothers. *20.5.1889:* Sank in the River St. Lawrence off Pointe aux Trembles, with the loss of eight lives after being in collision with the Allan Line steamship "POLYNESIAN" 2023/72, when on passage from Glasgow to Montreal with general cargo.

20. **TITANIA (1880-1886)** Iron steamship.
ON. 82333. 2,153g, 1,406n. 329.7 × 36.8 × 25.1 feet.
Compound inverted 2-cyl. steam engine of 460 N.H.P. made by the shipbuilder.
Fitted with passenger accommodation.
24.7.1880: Launched by D. & W. Henderson & Co., Glasgow (Yard No. 212) for Donaldson Brothers. *9.1880:* Completed. *3.11.1886:* Stranded near Charlton Point, Anticosti Island, Gulf of St. Lawrence while on passage from Glasgow to Montreal, with general cargo. *14.11.1886:* Abandoned to the insurance underwriters but later refloated and sold by the underwriters to Navigazione Generale Italiana, Italy. *1887:* Renamed PO. *1894:* Fitted with new boilers. *1910:* Sold to S.A. Nazionale di Servizi Marittimi, Italy. *1913:* Sold to Sicilia Societa di Navigazione, Italy. *1923:* Broken up in Italy.

CONCORDIA, as built *Company Archives*

21. **CONCORDIA (I) (1881-1909)** Iron steamship.
ON. 84342. 2,544g, 1,617n. 319.6 × 41.0 × 25.1 feet.
Compound inverted 2-cyl. steam engine of 285 N.H.P. made by the shipbuilder.
7.1881: Launched by Barclay, Curle & Co., Glasgow (Yard No. 301) for Donaldson Brothers. *8.1881:* Completed. *5.1894:* Fitted with new boilers. *7.1896:* Sustained ice damage when on passage from Glasgow to Montreal. *6.1909:* Sold to N. G. Pittaluga, Genoa and broken up in Italy.

CONCORDIA after being reboilered *Scottish Maritime Museum*

ALCIDES *Scottish Maritime Museum*

22. **ALCIDES (1886-1909)** Steel steamship.
ON. 93254. 3,421g, 2,181n. 340.0 × 42.1 × 30.0 feet.
Triple expansion 3-cyl. steam engine of 360 N.H.P. made by J. & J. Thomson, Glasgow.
6.2.1886: Launched by Napier, Shanks & Bell, Glasgow (Yard No. 33) for Donaldson Brothers. *17.12.1887:* Sustained damage when in collision with Allan Line steamship "MANITOBAN" 2,975/65. *11.1909:* Sold to The Shipbreaking Co. Ltd., and was scrapped at Glasgow.

23. **GLAMIS CASTLE/CIRCE (1887-1891)** Iron steamship.
ON. 68099. 2,364g, 1,559n. 331.9 × 35.7 × 26.4 feet.
Compound inverted direct acting 2-cyl. steam engine of 300 N.H.P. made by Rait & Lindsay, Glasgow; replaced 1888/89 by a triple expansion 3-cyl. steam engine made by Barclay, Curle & Co. Ltd., Glasgow.
20.2.1874: Launched by Aitken & Mansel, Glasgow as GLAMIS CASTLE for Thomas Skinner & Co., Glasgow. *8.1887:* Bought by Donaldson Brothers and in *1888* renamed CIRCE. *1888:* Re-engined. *18.7.1891:* Wrecked on East Cape, Anticosti Island, Gulf of St. Lawrence, with the loss of five lives, while on passage from Glasgow to Montreal with general cargo.

24. **WARWICK (1889-1896)** Steel steamship.
ON. 85805. 2,530g, 1,648n. 316.0 × 41.2 × 24.4 feet.
Compound inverted 2-cyl. steam engine of 350 N.H.P. made by the shipbuilder.
17.5.1882: Launched by Wigham Richardson & Co., Newcastle-upon-Tyne (Yard No. 140) as WARWICK for Great Western Steamship Co. Ltd., Bristol. *7.1889:* Bought by Donaldson Brothers. *30.12.1896:* Wrecked on Murr Ledges, Grand Manan Island, Bay of Fundy, Canada, when on passage from Glasgow to St. John, N.B., with a cargo of coal and general. All crew members were rescued.

25. **AMARYNTHIA (1890-1902)** Steel steamship.
ON. 84196. 4,012g, 2,612n. 400.5 × 42.2 × 29.7 feet.
Compound inverted 2-cyl. steam engine of 445 N.H.P. made by the shipbuilder.
22.12.1881: Launched by Gourlay Bros. & Co., Dundee (Yard No. 109) as MERTON HALL for Alexander & Radcliffe, Liverpool. *1882:* Owners became Robert Alexander

AMARYNTHIA *Company Archives*

& Co., Liverpool. *1883:* Transferred to Sun Shipping Co. Ltd., Liverpool. *4.1890:* Bought by Donaldson Brothers and renamed AMARYNTHIA. *1902:* Sold to Bruzzo Brothers, Italy and in *2.1902* broken up at Genoa.

26. INDRANI (1892-1915) Steel steamship.
ON. 93798. 3,640g, 2,339n. 361.8 × 44.3 × 27.1 feet.
Triple expansion 3-cyl. steam engine of 348 N.H.P. made by Fawcett, Preston & Co., Liverpool.
5.1888: Launched by T. Royden & Sons, Liverpool (Yard No. 248) as INDRANI for "Indrani" Steamship Co. Ltd. (Macvicar, Marshall & Co., managers), Liverpool. *8.1888:* Completed. *4.1892:* Bought by Donaldson Brothers. *4.1909:* Fitted with new boilers. *1913:* Transferred to Donaldson Line Ltd. (Donaldson Bros. Ltd., managers). *27.6.1915:* Captured by the German submarine U24 40 miles west of the Smalls Light, Wales, when on passage from Glasgow to Montreal, torpedoed and sunk.

INDRANI *Scottish Maritime Museum*

HESTIA   *Company Archives*

27. HESTIA (1893-1909) Steel steamship.
ON. 98053. 3,790g, 2,434n. 365.0 × 44.2 × 19.4 feet.
Triple expansion 3-cyl. steam engine of 390 N.H.P. made by the shipbuilder.
23.1.1890: Launched by William Doxford & Sons, Sunderland (Yard No. 193) as the MARY BEYTS for Bombay-London Steamship Co. Ltd. (Beyts & Craig, managers), London. *3.1890:* Completed. *2.1893:* Bought by Donaldson Brothers and renamed HESTIA. *25.10.1909:* Wrecked, with the loss of 35 lives, on Old Proprietor Ledges, Grand Manan Island, Bay of Fundy, Canada while on passage from Glasgow to St. John N.B. with a cargo of general and livestock.

TRITONIA   *Company Archives*

28. TRITONIA (I) (1893-1914) Steel steamship.
ON. 99890. 4,272g, 2,720n. 377.0 × 46.1 × 28.0 feet.
Triple expansion 3-cyl. steam engine of 411 N.H.P. made by the shipbuilder.
19.1.1893: Launched by D. & W. Henderson & Co., Glasgow (Yard No. 364), for Donaldson Brothers. *4.1893:* Completed. *1913:* Transferred to Donaldson Line Ltd., (Donaldson Bros. Ltd., managers). *19.12.1914:* Mined and sunk 22 miles N.N.E. of Tory Island, Ireland, while on passage from Manchester to St. John, N.B., with a cargo of coal. The mine was one of a spread laid by the German minelayer "BERLIN".

ORTHIA   *Courtesy "Sea Breezes"*

29. ORTHIA (1896-1922) Steel steamship.
ON. 106012. 4,225g, 2,694n. 377.0 × 46.6 × 19.0 feet.
Triple expansion 3-cyl. steam engine of 404 N.H.P. made by G. Clark Ltd., Sunderland.
28.4.1896: Launched by J. Laing, Sunderland (Yard No. 538) for Donaldson Brothers.
6.1896: Completed. *1913:* Transferred to the Donaldson Line Ltd. (Donaldson Bros. Ltd., managers). *11.10.1913:* When berthed at Sheerness discharging a cargo of wood pulp from Botwood, Newfoundland, a serious fire broke out in the engine room and spread to the hold aft of this area, causing considerable damage to the cargo remaining in this hold. A fire fighting team from H.M.S. "VENGEANCE" rendered assistance along with the crew of the tug "DILIGENT". The fire was extinguished and discharge of the cargo completed. Due to the engineroom being badly damaged the ORTHIA was towed to London where repairs were carried out. *5.7.1922:* While on passage from Avonmouth to Montreal collided with the British steamship "AIREDALE", 3,044/99 in the St. Lawrence River and was beached at Sorel. *15.7.1922:* Refloated, but in *9.1922* declared a constructive total loss and sold to C. J. Sewell, Quebec, and broken up.

30. KEEMUN (1897-1900) Steel steamship.
ON. 98189. 3,132g, 1,985n. 361.6 × 41.7 × 24.5 feet.
Triple expansion 3-cyl. steam engine of 442 N.H.P. made by J. Dickinson, Sunderland.
30.9.1890: Launched by J. L. Thompson & Sons, Sunderland (Yard No. 267) as KEEMUN for China Mutual Steam Navigation Co. Ltd. (A. Holt & Co., managers), Liverpool. *11.1890:* Completed. *1.1897:* Bought by Donaldson Brothers. *8.1900:* Sold to F. Schepens & G. Tonnelier, Belgium and renamed PATRIE. *1901:* Sold to J. H. Andressen, Successores, Portugal and renamed PATRIA. *1906:* Sold to G. S. Patrikios Fils, Greece and renamed PATRICIA. *18.1.1907:* Sank after being in collision with the Norwegian steamship "MORINGEN" 568/71 seven miles from Haisboro' Light when on passage from Hull to Alexandria, Egypt with a cargo of coal.

31. KASTALIA (I) (1897-1916) Steel steamship.
ON. 106094. 4,039g, 2,562n. 377.0 × 46.6 × 18.8 feet.
Triple expansion 3-cyl. steam engine of 395 N.H.P. made by the shipbuilder.
2.6.1897: Launched by The London & Glasgow Engineering & Iron Shipbuilding Co. Ltd., Glasgow (Yard No. 291) for Donaldson Brothers. *7.1897:* Completed. *1913:* Transferred to Donaldson Line Ltd. (Donaldson Bros. Ltd., managers). *3.1916:* Sold to Equinox Steamship Co. Ltd. (Leopold Walford (London) Ltd. managers), London and renamed YONNE. *6.4.1916:* Torpedoed and sunk 18 miles N.N.W. of Cherchel, Algeria in a position 36.52N 02.00E by the German submarine U34 when on passage from the Clyde to Alexandria and New Caledonia with a cargo of coal and coke.

SALACIA　　　　　　　　　　　　　　　　　　　　　　　　　　*Company Archives*

32. SALACIA (I) (1898-1912) Steel steamship.
ON. 108747. 4,134g, 2,636n. 390.0 × 46.0 × 20.6 feet.
Triple expansion 3-cyl. steam engine of 501 N.H.P. made by Dunsmuir & Jackson, Glasgow.
5.7.1895: Launched by Charles Connell & Co., Glasgow (Yard No. 222) as MANILA for Pinillos, Izquierdo y Cia, Spain. *8.1895:* Completed. *7.1898:* Bought by Donaldson Brothers and renamed SALACIA. *2.1912:* Sold to M. Jebsen, Germany. *1913:* Sold to Tito Campanella, Italy and in *1915* renamed QUARTO. *6.2.1915:* Purchased by the Italian Navy. *20.2.1915-5.1915:* Converted by the Royal Naval Yard at Spezia for service as a seaplane tender and submarine depot ship and renamed EUROPA. *10.9.1920:* Withdrawn from service and subsequently scrapped in Italy.

SALACIA as the seaplane tender **EUROPA**　　　　　　　　　　*Aldo Fraccaroli*

33. ALMORA (1899-1916) Steel steamship.
ON. 108790. 4,385g, 2,835n. 375.0 × 50.0 × 26.0 feet.
Triple expansion 3-cyl. steam engine of 368 N.H.P. made by the shipbuilder.
28.12.1898: Launched by D. & W. Henderson & Co., Glasgow (Yard No. 408) as ALMORA for Glasgow Navigation Co. Ltd. (Maclay and McIntyre, managers), Glasgow. *2.1899:* Completed. *21.11.1899:* Bought by Glasgow & Newport News Steamship Co. Ltd. (Donaldson Brothers, managers). *1913:* Transferred to Donaldson Line Ltd. (Donaldson Bros. Ltd. managers). *4.1916:* Sold to Houlder, Middleton & Co. Ltd., London. *2.10.1917:* Torpedoed and sunk by a submarine 100 miles W x N from Cape Spartel, Morocco in a position 35.45N 07.45W when on passage from Barry to Gibraltar.

34. LAKONIA (I) (1899-1924) Steel steamship.
ON. 111195. 4,686g, 3,046n. 401.7 × 49.2 × 28.1 feet.
Triple expansion 3-cyl. steam engine of 520 N.H.P. made by the shipbuilder.
24.4.1899: Launched by London & Glasgow Engineering & Iron Shipbuilding Co. Ltd., Glasgow (Yard No. 300) for Donaldson Brothers. *6.1899:* Completed. *1913:* Transferred to Donaldson Line Ltd. (Donaldson Bros. Ltd., managers). *4.1924:* Sold to A. Ardito, Italy, for scrapping at Genoa where she arrived on *14.5.1924*.

MARINA at Fowey   D. McKenzie

35. MARINA (II) (1900-1916) Steel steamship.
ON. 111291. 5,204g, 3,322n. 400.0 × 52.0 × 29.2 feet.
Triple expansion 3-cyl. steam engine of 510 N.H.P. made by Sir C. Furness, Westgarth & Co. Ltd., Middlesbrough.
29.5.1900: Launched by Furness, Withy & Co. Ltd., West Hartlepool (Yard No. 249) for Donaldson Brothers. *9.1900:* Completed. *1913:* Transferred to Donaldson Line Limited (Donaldson Bros. Ltd., managers). *28.10.1916:* Torpedoed and sunk with the loss of 18 lives, thirty miles west of Fastnet Rock, Ireland, by the German submarine U55 when on passage from Glasgow to Baltimore.

36. PARTHENIA (I) (1901-1917) Steel steamship.
ON. 113949. 5,160g, 3,310n. 400.5 × 52.1 × 29.3 feet.
Triple expansion 3-cyl. steam engine of 489 N.H.P. made by Richardsons, Westgarth & Co. Ltd., Hartlepool.
19.2.1901: Launched by Furness, Withy & Co. Ltd., West Hartlepool (Yard No. 254) for Donaldson Brothers. *5.1901:* Completed. Later in *1901* registered in the ownership of "Parthenia" S.S. Co. Ltd. (Donaldson Brothers, managers). *1913:* Transferred to Donaldson Line Ltd. (Donaldson Bros. Ltd., managers). *6.12.1913:* Departed from

Botwood N.F. bound for Manchester with a cargo of wood pulp. On *9.12.1913* the rudder was lost and the following day the Norwegian vessel "WAGAMA" 4,969/13 took the PARTHENIA in tow for St. Johns, N.F., arriving at a safe berth on *23.12.1913.* When drydocked in *1.1914* extensive damage was found. In addition to fitting a new rudder the stern frame was repaired along with some shell plating and the propeller had to be changed due to blade damage. The 1,500 tons of cargo discharged prior to drydocking to lighten ship was reloaded on completion of repair work and the voyage was resumed at the end of *2.1914. 6.6.1917:* Torpedoed and sunk by the German submarine U69 140 miles W by N of Bishop Rock, Scilly Isles, when on passage from New York to London. Three members of her crew were lost. Her cargo consisted mainly of steel and oats.

ATHENIA, as completed — Company Archives

37. ATHENIA (I) (1904-1917) Steel steamship.
ON. 119121. As built 7,830g, 5,133n. As rebuilt 8,668g, 5,523n.
478.0 × 56.0 × 32.5 feet.
Two triple expansion 3-cyl. steam engines of 855 N.H.P. made by the shipbuilder, driving twin screws.
Part refrigerated capacity.
20.10.1903: Launched by Vickers, Sons and Maxim Ltd., Barrow (Yard No. 288) for "Athenia" S.S. Co. Ltd. (Donaldson Brothers, managers). *3.1904:* Completed. *1905:* Converted to a passenger/cargo vessel with accommodation for 600 passengers. *1913:* Transferred to Donaldson Line Ltd. (Donaldson Bros. Ltd., managers). *1916:* Transferred to Anchor-Donaldson Ltd. (A. C. F. Henderson, manager). *16.8.1917:* Torpedoed and sunk by the German submarine U53, seven miles North of Inishtrahull Island, Ireland with the loss of nine crew members and six passengers, when on passage from Montreal to Glasgow with a general cargo.

ATHENIA, as rebuilt — W.S.S. Wylie collection

CASSANDRA   *W.S.S. Brownell collection*

38. CASSANDRA/CARMIA (I) (1906-1929) Steel steamship.
ON. 124130. As built 8,135g, 5,221n. As rebuilt 6,407g, 3,677n. 455.0 × 53.2 × 29.1 feet.
Two triple expansion 3-cyl. steam engines of 862 N.H.P. made by the shipbuilder driving twin screws.
Part refrigerated capacity.
27.6.1906: Launched by Scotts' Shipbuilding & Engineering Co. Ltd., Greenock (Yard No. 408) as CASSANDRA for "Cassandra" S.S. Co. Ltd. (Donaldson Brothers, managers). *9.1906:* Completed. *12.1913:* Transferred to Donaldson Line Ltd. (Donaldson Bros. Ltd. managers). *12.1916:* Transferred to Anchor-Donaldson Ltd. (A. C. F. Henderson, manager). In *1917* the joint managers became Donaldson Bros. Ltd., and Anchor Line (Henderson Bros.) Ltd. *9.1925:* Transferred to Donaldson Line Ltd., (Donaldson Bros. Ltd. managers) and converted from a passenger vessel to a livestock and general cargo carrier. Renamed CARMIA. *12.1929:* Sold to A. Bernstein, Germany and renamed DRACHENSTEIN. *1934:* Broken up at Kiel by Deutsche Werke A.G.

PYTHIA, as **RAGLAN CASTLE**   *National Maritime Museum*

39. PYTHIA (1910-1911) Steel steamship.
ON. 108187. 4,239g, 2,722n. 383.5 × 46.3 × 20.0 feet.
Triple expansion 3-cyl. steam engine of 419 N.H.P. made by the shipbuilder.
20.1.1897: Launched by Barclay, Curle & Co. Ltd., Glasgow (Yard No. 408) as RAGLAN CASTLE for Castle Mail Packets Co. Ltd. (D. Currie & Co., managers) London. *3.1897:* Completed. *1900:* Transferred to Union-Castle Mail S.S. Co. Ltd., (D. Currie & Co., managers). *1904:* Sold back to Barclay, Curle & Co. Ltd. *2.1905:* Sold to A/S Det Ostasiatiske Kompagni, Denmark, and renamed ST. DOMINGO. *1908:* Sold back to Barclay, Curle & Co. Ltd., and in *1909* reverted to the name RAGLAN CASTLE. *1.1910:* Bought by "Pythia" S.S. Co. Ltd., (Donaldson Brothers, managers) and renamed PYTHIA. *11.1911:* Sold to Akties. Dominion Whaling Co. Ltd., (T. Dannevig & Co., managers) Norway and converted to a whale oil refinery. *1919:* Chr. Christensen jnr., appointed manager. *1920:* Sold to A/S Odd (Chr. Christensen jnr., manager) Norway. *1922:* Transferred to Hvalfangerakties, Odd (I. Bryde and L. Thorsen, managers) Norway. *18.4.1929:* Capsized while under-going repairs at Framnes Mek Verksted A/S., Sandefjord. Subsequently taken over by Framnes M.V. and repaired. *1930:* Sold to Hvalfanger A/S Africa (B. Gundersen, manager) Norway and renamed READY. Management subsequently transferred to Frithjof Bettum. *4.6.1931:* Arrived at Tonsberg and laid up. *12.7.1934:* Sold to Metal Industries Ltd., for £6,500. *7.9.1934:* Left Sandefjord in tow for Rosyth for scrapping. *3.10.1934:* Demolition commenced.

SATURNIA   W.S.P.L.

40. SATURNIA (1910-1928) Steel steamship.
ON. 129489. 8,611g, 5,494n. 456.3 × 55.3 × 29.1 feet.
Two triple expansion 3-cyl. steam engines of 872 N.H.P. made by Dunsmuir & Jackson Ltd., Glasgow, driving twin screws.
Part refrigerated capacity.
29.3.1910: Launched by C. Connell & Co. Ltd., Glasgow (Yard No. 333) for "Saturnia" S.S. Co. Ltd., (Donaldson Brothers, managers). *6.1910:* Completed. *1913:* Transferred to Donaldson Line Ltd., (Donaldson Bros. Ltd., managers). *1916:* Transferred to Anchor-Donaldson Ltd. (A. C. F. Henderson, manager). *1917:* Joint managers became Donaldson Bros. Ltd., and Anchor Line (Henderson Bros.) Ltd. *1928:* Sold to Cantieri Metallurgici Della Venezia Giulia S.A., Italy and broken up at Genoa.

LETITIA *Courtesy "Sea Breezes"*

41. LETITIA (I) (1912-1917) Steel steamship.
ON. 133033. 8,991g, 5,764n. 470.4 × 56.9 × 28.8 feet.
Two triple expansion 3-cyl. steam engines of 962 N.H.P. made by the shipbuilder, driving twin screws.
Part refrigerated capacity.
20.2.1912: Launched by Scotts' Shipbuilding & Engineering Co. Ltd., Greenock (Yard No. 437) for "Letitia" S.S. Co. Ltd. (Donaldson Brothers, managers). *4.1912:* Completed. *1913:* Transferred to Donaldson Line Ltd. (Donaldson Bros. Ltd., managers). *1916:* Transferred to Anchor-Donaldson Ltd. (A. C. F. Henderson, manager). *1917:* Joint managers became Donaldson Bros. Ltd. and Anchor Line (Henderson Bros.) Ltd. *1.8.1917:* Whilst operating as a hospital ship went aground on Chebucto Head, Halifax, N.S. and was abandoned as a constructive total loss. She was on passage from Liverpool to Halifax N.S. with 546 patients, 84 medical staff and 137 crew, all of whom were saved except one crew member who lost his life.

LETITIA aground on Chebucto Head, 8.1917 *National Maritime Museum*

60

LIVONIAN as LUDGATE HILL   W.S.S. Brownell collection

42. LIVONIAN (1913) Steel steamship. (Donaldson had nominal control only).
ON. 84195. 4,017g, 2,594n. 420.3 × 47.0 × 26.5 feet.
Two compound inverted 2-cyl. steam engines of 600 N.H.P. made by J. Howden & Co., Glasgow driving twin screws, replaced in *1900* by two triple expansion 3-cyl. steam engines of 312 N.H.P. made and fitted by Workman, Clark & Co. Ltd., Belfast, driving twin screws.
11.1881: Launched by Dobie & Co., Glasgow (Yard No. 114) as LUDGATE HILL for S.S. Ludgate Hill Co. Ltd. (W. B. Hill and W. H. Nott, managers) London. *9.6.1897:* Sold to Allan Line Steamship Co. Ltd. (J. & A. Allan, managers) Glasgow and *30.7.1897* renamed LIVONIAN. *1900:* Fitted with new engines and boilers by Workman, Clark & Co. Ltd., Belfast. *1909:* Managers became Allan Brothers & Co. U.K. Ltd. *1913:* Passed to Donaldson Brothers Ltd. who took nominal control of the vessel while a dispute over a contract went to arbitration. *1913:* Donaldson Brothers won the case with control of the vessel to remain with Allan Line. Vessel continued to operate services to the River Plate until *28.3.1914* when she was laid up at Gareloch with a view to being sold for scrap. This plan was cancelled and she was sold to the Admiralty on *7.11.1914* for use as a block ship at Dover Harbour Western Entrance. (The ship's register was closed *10.12.1914*). *1933:* Remains removed.

43. ONTARIAN/CABOTIA (I) (1913-1916) Steel steamship.
ON. 111273. 4,309g, 2,780n. 385.2 × 48.8 × 26.9 feet.
Triple expansion 3-cyl. steam engine of 359 N.H.P. made by Rankin & Blackmore, Greenock.
Ordered by Raeburn & Verel, Glasgow, from Robert Duncan & Co. Ltd., Port Glasgow, (Yard No. 291) but sold on the stocks to Allan Line Steamship Co. Ltd. (J. & A. Allan, managers) Glasgow. *16.5.1900:* Launched as ONTARIAN. *7.1900:* Completed. *1909:* Managers became Allan Bros. & Co. U.K. Ltd. *19.11.1913:* Bought by Donaldson Line Ltd., (Donaldson Bros. Ltd., managers) and in *2.1914* renamed CABOTIA. *20.10.1916:* Intercepted by the German submarine U69 when 120 miles W.N.W. from Tory Island, Ireland, during a voyage from Montreal to Manchester and sunk by gunfire. Thirty two members of her crew, including the Master, were lost.

44. ORCADIAN/POLARIA (1914-1916) Steel steamship.
ON. 102644. 3,546g, 2,252n. 361.0 × 44.4 × 26.2 feet.
Triple expansion 3-cyl. steam engine of 328 N.H.P. made by the shipbuilder.
24.10.1893: Launched by Workman, Clark & Co. Ltd., Belfast (Yard No. 105) as ORMISTON for R. & C. Allan, Glasgow. *11.1893:* Completed. *16.12.1898:* Sold to Allan Line Steamship Co. Ltd. (J. & A. Allan, managers), Glasgow and renamed ORCADIAN. *9.1909:* Managers became Allan Bros. & Co. U.K. Ltd. *26.9.1914:* Bought by Donaldson Line Ltd. (Donaldson Bros. Ltd., managers) and in *11.1915* renamed POLARIA. *24.3.1916:* Sold to Houlder, Middleton & Co. Ltd., London. *5.1.1918:* When on passage from Cardiff to Alexandria, Egypt with a cargo of coal and wagons, grounded near El Rot, Alexandria and was wrecked.

45. CLUTHA (1915-1917) Steel steamship.
ON. 98897. 3,426g, 2,171n. 328.4 × 42.3 × 21.4 feet.
Quadruple expansion 4-cyl. steam engine of 261 N.H.P. made by the shipbuilder.
13.12.1890: Launched by Wigham Richardson & Co., Newcastle-upon-Tyne, (Yard No. 255) as HOLKAR for G. Tweedy & Son, London. *2.1891:* Completed. *7.1893:* Sold to London Steamers Ltd. (P. W. Richardson, manager), London. *10.1897:* Sold to Hungarian Levant S.S. Co. Ltd., Fiume, Austria-Hungary and renamed ATTILA. *24.8.1914:* Intercepted by the Royal Navy off the Shetland Islands whilst on passage from Port Talbot to Bergen in ballast, and escorted to Kirkwall. Condemned as a prize. *5.1915:* Bought from the Admiralty by Donaldson Line Ltd. (Donaldson Bros. Ltd., managers) and renamed CLUTHA. *9.1917:* Sold to The Shipping Controller (W. Robertson, manager), London. *1921:* Sold to Levante Soc. di Nav. Marittima, Italy. *1923:* Taken over by the Italian Government and later in *1923* sold to Cantieri Navali ed Acciaiere di Venezia and broken up in Italy.

ORMIDALE

R. J. McCormick

46. ORMIDALE (1915-1919) Steel steamship.
ON. 102625. 3,560g, 2,305n. 361.0 × 44.5 × 26.5 feet.
Triple expansion 3-cyl. steam engine of 369 N.H.P. made by the shipbuilder.
17.8.1893: Launched by Workman, Clark & Co. Ltd., Belfast (Yard No. 98) as ORMIDALE for R. & C. Allan, Glasgow. *9.1893:* Completed. *19.5.1915:* Bought by Donaldson Line Ltd. (Donaldson Bros. Ltd., managers). *15.4.1919:* Sold to S. Vlassopulos, Greece and renamed ISTROS. *1925:* Sold to M. N. Filinis (P. G. Callimanopulos, manager), Greece. *1930:* Sold to Italian shipbreakers and broken up at Savona.

47. MERCURIA (1915-1919) Steel steamship.
ON. 111222. 3,092g, 1,938n. 333.0 × 45.0 × 15.9 feet.
Triple expansion 3-cyl. steam engine of 343 N.H.P. made by D. Rowan & Co., Glasgow.
30.5.1899: Launched by A. McMillan & Son Ltd., Dumbarton (Yard No. 366) as KELVINGROVE for the Glasgow Steam Shipping Co. Ltd. (J. Black & Co., managers) Glasgow. *10.1899:* Completed. *7.1915:* Bought by Donaldson Line Ltd. (Donaldson

MERCURIA as KELVINGROVE *University of Glasgow Archives*

Bros. Ltd., managers) and renamed MERCURIA. *1919:* Sold to Letricheux Line Ltd. (Letricheux & David Ltd., managers), Swansea. *7.1920:* Sold to Brynymor Steamship Co. Ltd., (Letricheux & David Ltd., managers), Swansea. *8.1922:* Sold to Pridmore & Roe, Swansea. *3.1926:* Sold to M. G. Nicolich, Brazil and renamed INES. *1933:* Sold to Carlos Ozorio, Brazil and renamed CARUARU. *1934:* Sold to Cia. Carbonifera Rio Grandense, Brazil and renamed CAXIAS. *1943:* Sold to Compania Commercio e Navegacao, Brazil. *1957:* Sold to Navegacao Mercantil S.A., Brazil. *1961:* Reported scrapped.

CRANLEY at Fowey *D. McKenzie*

48. CRANLEY (1915-1931) Steel steamship.
ON. 118257. 4,644g, 2,903n. 390.0 × 51.5 × 26.5 feet.
Triple expansion 3-cyl. steam engine of 455 N.H.P. made by the shipbuilder.
28.2.1903: Launched by D. & W. Henderson & Co. Ltd., Glasgow (Yard No. 432) as CRANLEY for Century Shipping Co. Ltd. (Harris & Dixon Ltd., managers), London. *3.1903:* Completed. *1906:* Sold to Cie. Belge d'Armement et de Transport Maritimes Soc. Anon., Belgium and renamed CAMETA. *1908:* Sold back to Century Shipping Co. Ltd. (Harris & Dixon Ltd., managers) London and renamed CRANLEY. *7.1915:* Bought by Anglo-Newfoundland Steamship Co. Ltd. (Donaldson Bros. Ltd., managers). *1916:* Transferred to Anglo-Newfoundland Development Co. Ltd. (Donaldson Bros. Ltd., managers). *8.1.1931:* Sold for £4,000 to T. W. Ward Ltd., for demolition at Briton Ferry, where she arrived *15.1.1931.*

49. ALCONDA (1915-1924) Steel steamship.
ON. 124014. 4,298g, 2,695n. 381.0 × 49.0 × 25.7 feet.
Triple expansion 3-cyl. steam engine of 421 N.H.P. made by G. Clark, Sunderland.
3.10.1906: Launched by W. Pickersgill & Sons, Sunderland (Yard No. 156) as ALCONDA for E. F. & W. Roberts, Liverpool. *11.1906:* Completed. *1911:* Transferred to Ardova Steamship Co. Ltd. (E. F. & W. Roberts, managers), Liverpool. *7.1915:* Bought by Anglo-Newfoundland Steamship Co. Ltd. (Donaldson Bros. Ltd. managers). *1916:* Transferred to Anglo-Newfoundland Development Co. Ltd. (Donaldson Bros. Ltd., managers). *12.1924:* Sold for £19,000 to Essex Line Ltd., (Meldrum & Swinson, managers) London and renamed ESSEX GLADE. *5.1935:* Sold to Italian shipbreakers for £6,600 for demolition at Venice.

50. TRITONIA (II) (1915-1917) Steel steamship.
ON. 122802. 4,445g, 2,846n. 380.3 × 49.7 × 26.9 feet.
Triple expansion 3-cyl. steam engine of 457 N.H.P. made by the shipbuilder.
11.9.1905: Launched by Scotts' Shipbuilding & Engineering Co. Ltd., Greenock (Yard No. 395) as GULISTAN for the Anglo-Algerian Steamship Co. (1896) Ltd., (F. C. Strick & Co. Ltd., managers), Swansea. *10.1905:* Completed. *1912:* Transferred to Strick Line Ltd. (F. C. Strick & Co. Ltd., managers), London. *6.1913:* Sold to Borderdale Shipping Co. Ltd. (J. Little & Co. (Glasgow) Ltd., managers), Glasgow and renamed BORDERDALE. *10.1915:* Bought by Donaldson Line Ltd., (Donaldson Bros. Ltd., managers) and renamed TRITONIA. *26.2.1917:* Torpedoed and sunk by the German submarine U49, 20 miles N.W. by W from Tearagh Island, Ireland, when on passage from St. John N.B. and Halifax N.S. to Glasgow with a general cargo and a consignment of horses. Two members of the crew were lost.

ARGALIA as SWANLEY   *W.S.S. Brownell collection*

51. ARGALIA (I) (1917) Steel steamship.
ON. 118288. 4,641g, 2,908n. 390.0 × 51.5 × 26.5 feet.
Triple expansion 3-cyl. steam engine of 455 N.H.P. made by the shipbuilder.
28.4.1903: Launched by D. & W. Henderson & Co. Ltd., Glasgow (Yard No. 433) as SWANLEY for Century Shipping Co. Ltd. (Harris & Dixon Ltd., managers) London. *6.1903:* Completed. *2.1917:* Bought by Donaldson Line Ltd. (Donaldson Bros. Ltd., managers) and renamed ARGALIA. *6.8.1917:* Torpedoed and sunk by the German submarine U94, 81 miles N.W. by W. from Tory Island, Ireland in a position 55.35N 10.35W when on passage from Baltimore to Glasgow with a general cargo including a consignment of horses. Three members of the crew were lost.

SALACIA *W.S.S. Brownell collection*

52. DUNACHTON/SALACIA (II) (1917-1936) Steel steamship.
ON. 129418. 5,201g, 3,311n. 410.5 × 52.3 × 28.6 feet.
Triple expansion 3-cyl. steam engine of 536 N.H.P. made by Dunsmuir & Jackson Ltd., Glasgow.
24.9.1912: Launched by Charles Connell & Co. Ltd., Glasgow (Yard No. 348) as DUNACHTON for Dunedin Steamship Co. Ltd. (Henderson & McIntosh, managers) Leith. *10.1912:* Completed. *7.1917:* Bought for £180,000 by Donaldson Line Ltd. (Donaldson Bros. Ltd., managers). *1919:* Renamed SALACIA. *9.1936:* Sold for £14,000 to Townsend Brothers (Shipping) Ltd., London and in *12.1936* resold to Ding Yao Dung (Seiichi Okada, manager), Chefoo, China and renamed SHENG YU. *1938:* Sold to Kuribayashi Shosen K.K., Japan and renamed ZUISYO MARU. *1939:* Sold to Kyodo Kaiun K.K., Japan. *14.8.1944:* Torpedoed and sunk by the United States submarine "RAY" off the coast of Sarawak in position 03.52N 112.56E.

CONCORDIA *W.S.P.L.*

53. GRETAVALE/CONCORDIA (II) (1917-1934) Steel steamship.
ON. 137830. 5,388g, 3,418n. 410.2 × 53.5 × 28.4 feet.
Triple expansion 3-cyl. steam engine of 485 N.H.P. made by J. G. Kincaid & Co. Ltd., Greenock.
29.11.1916: Launched by Greenock & Grangemouth Dockyard Co. Ltd., Greenock (Yard No. 369) as GRETAVALE for Vale Steamship Co. Ltd. (Barr, Crombie & Co., managers) Glasgow. *1.1917:* Completed. *10.1917:* Bought by Donaldson Line Ltd. (Donaldson Bros. Ltd., managers). *1919:* Renamed CONCORDIA. *5.3.1934:* When on passage from St. John N.B. and Halifax N.S., to Glasgow, she was involved in a collision with the United States steamship "BLACK EAGLE" 5,060/20 and sank about 40 miles S.E. of Sable Island, N.S. in position 43.11N 59.11W. All hands were rescued by the American vessel and taken to the United States for repatriation. The CONCORDIA had on board a full general cargo and about 400 head of cattle at the time of her loss.

PARTHENIA   *J. Clarkson*

54. KIRKHOLM/PARTHENIA (II) (1918-1940) Steel steamship.
ON. 137847. 4,753g, 3,063n. 399.7 × 51.9 × 26.9 feet.
Triple expansion 3-cyl. steam engine of 488 N.H.P. made by D. Rowan & Co., Glasgow.
4.1917: Launched by Russell & Co., Port Glasgow (Yard No. 686) as KIRKHOLM for Kirkholm Steamship Co. Ltd. (J. R. Cuthbertson & Co., managers), Glasgow. *6.1917:* Completed. *25.4.1918:* Bought by Donaldson Line Ltd. (Donaldson Bros. Ltd., managers). *1919:* Renamed PARTHENIA. *27.6.1938:* Managers became Donaldson Bros. & Black Ltd. *29.11.1940:* When on passage in Convoy No. HX88 from Montreal to Glasgow was involved in collision with the British motor tanker "ROBERT F. HAND", 12,197/33, which was in the same convoy, and sank seven miles S.W. of Sanda Light in the approaches to the Firth of Clyde. One life was lost.

ARGALIA   *National Maritime Museum*

55. ARGALIA (II) (1919-1927) Steel steamship.
ON. 142474. 5,214g, 3,186n. 400.1 × 52.3 × 28.5 feet.
Triple expansion 3-cyl. steam engine of 517 N.H.P. made by Blair & Co. Ltd., Stockton.
27.5.1918: Launched by Craig, Taylor & Co. Ltd., Stockton (Yard No. 199) as WAR KESTREL for The Shipping Controller. *7.1918:* Completed and Harris & Dixon Ltd., London, appointed managers. *4.1919:* Bought by Donaldson Line Ltd. (Donaldson Bros. Ltd., managers) and renamed ARGALIA. *6.1927:* Sold to Tatsuuma Kisen K.K., Japan and renamed MIYADONO MARU (owners name was later rendered Tatuuma Kisen K.K. following the revision of the Japanese language). *19.6.1943:* Torpedoed and sunk by the United States submarine "GROWLER" 250 miles north of Mussau Island, New Guinea, in a position 01.38N 148.14E.

CHALISTER as HODUR   W.S.P.L.

56. CHALISTER (1919-1920) Steel steamship.
ON. 135329. 5,344g, 3,369n. 425.6 × 54.6 × 25.9 feet.
Triple expansion 3-cyl. steam engine of 470 N.H.P. made by the shipbuilder.
2.7.1913: Launched by D. & W. Henderson & Co. Ltd., Glasgow (Yard No. 484) as CHALISTER for Chalister Steamship Co. Ltd. (A. H. & E. Gunn, managers), Cardiff. *8.1913:* Completed. *8.1919:* Bought by Anglo-Newfoundland Development Co. Ltd. (Donaldson Bros. Ltd., managers). *1.1920:* Sold to R. A. McLelland, Kingston, Ontario, Canada. *10.1922:* Sold to Adams Bros. Ltd., Aberdeen. *11.1924:* Sold for £47,500 to Turnbull, Scott Shipping Co. Ltd. (Turnbull, Scott & Co., managers), London and renamed HAGGERSGATE. *3.1936:* Sold for £21,250 to Seereederei "Frigga" A.G., Germany and renamed HODUR. *20.4.1942:* Torpedoed and sunk by H.M. submarine "TRIDENT" off Namsos, Norway in position 64.38N 10.54E.

CABOTIA   W.S.S. Brownell collection

57. CABOTIA (II) (1919-1925) Steel steamship.
ON. 142323. 5,160g, 3,122n. 400.4 × 52.3 × 28.4 feet.
Triple expansion 3-cyl. steam engine of 518 N.H.P. made by the shipbuilder.
14.2.1918: Launched by Harland & Wolff Ltd., Belfast (Yard No. 531) as WAR VIPER for The Shipping Controller. *3.1918:* Completed and G. Heyn & Sons, Belfast, appointed managers. *8.1919:* Bought by Donaldson Line Ltd. (Donaldson Bros. Ltd., managers) and renamed CABOTIA. *1920:* Transferred to Anchor-Donaldson Ltd. (Donaldson Bros. Ltd. and Anchor Line (Henderson Bros.) Ltd., joint managers). *2.1925:* Sold to Court Line Ltd. (Haldin & Co. Ltd., managers), London and renamed CEDRINGTON COURT. *1929:* Transferred to United British S.S. Co. Ltd. (Haldin & Philipps Ltd., managers) London. *1936:* Transferred to Court Line Ltd. (Haldin & Philipps Ltd., managers) London. *7.1.1940:* Mined and sunk two miles N.E. of the North Goodwin Light Vessel, southern North Sea in a position 51.23N 01.35E, when on passage from Buenos Aires to Hull with a cargo of bulk wheat. All her crew were saved.

TRITONIA　　　　　　　　　　　　　　　　　　　　　　　　　　　　　R. S. Craig

58. TRITONIA (III) (1919-1929) Steel steamship.
ON. 142616. 5,244g, 3,194n. 400.5 × 52.3 × 28.5 feet.
Triple expansion 3-cyl. steam engine of 517 N.H.P. made by the shipbuilder.
29.6.1918: Launched by Caird & Co. Ltd., Greenock (Yard No. 352) as WAR EMU for The Shipping Controller. *8.1918:* Completed and Donaldson Bros. Ltd. appointed managers. *10.1919:* Bought by Donaldson Line Ltd. (Donaldson Bros. Ltd., managers) and renamed TRITONIA. *28.2.1929:* Lost by explosion and fire when working cargo at the anchorage in Buenaventura harbour, Colombia. She was on a voyage from Vancouver and Los Angeles to Callao with general cargo which included a large consignment of explosives. Two lives were lost in the incident.

KASTALIA　　　　　　　　　　　　　　　　　　　　　　　　　　　　　W.S.P.L.

59. KASTALIA (II) (1919-1936) Steel steamship.
ON. 141923. 4,663g, 2,886n. 384.9 × 52.0 × 26.7 feet.
Triple expansion 3-cyl. steam engine of 517 N.H.P. made by Rankin & Blackmore Ltd., Greenock.
27.8.1919: Launched by Lithgows Ltd., Port Glasgow (Yard No. 726) for Donaldson Line Ltd. (Donaldson Bros. Ltd., managers). *10.1919:* Completed. *9.1936:* Sold for £17,000 to Ogmore Steamship Co. Ltd. (Ships Finance & Management Co. Ltd., managers) London and renamed TUSKER ROCK. *8.1937:* Sold to Yannaghas Bros. & Co., Greece and renamed ARMATHIA. *22.10.1949:* Reported detained by Chinese Nationalists. *1951:* Reported as trading normally. *1952:* Sold to Cia de Vapores Costa Rica, Costa Rica and renamed CAPTAIN ANTONIOS K. *1.3.1954:* When on passage from Newport, Mon., to Taranto, Italy with coal, developed leaks and sank off Algeria in a position 37.05N 07.53E. All her crew of 17 were picked up by the Strick steamship "NIGARISTAN", 7,173/47.

CORRIENTES   *J. Clarkson*

60. CORRIENTES (I) (1920-1940) Steel steamship.
ON. 144218. 6,863g, 4,233n. 419.0 × 54.8 × 35.7 feet.
Three steam turbines of 756 N.H.P. made by Parsons Marine Steam Turbine Co. Ltd., Newcastle-upon-Tyne, double reduction geared to a single screw shaft.
Fully refrigerated capacity.
22.1.1920: Launched by Short Bros. Ltd., Sunderland (Yard No. 397) for Donaldson South American Line Ltd. (Donaldson Bros. Ltd., managers). *7.1920:* Completed. *27.6.1938:* Managers became Donaldson Bros. & Black Ltd. *26.9.1940:* Torpedoed by the German submarine U32 and abandoned by her crew. However, she remained afloat until *28.9.1940* when U37 sank her with torpedoes and gunfire in a position 53.49N 24.19W. She was on a voyage from Glasgow to Montreal with general cargo.

CORDILLERA   *J. Clarkson*

61. CORDILLERA (1920-1948) Steel steamship.
ON. 144239. 6,865g, 4,248n. 419.0 × 54.8 × 35.7 feet.
Three steam turbines of 756 N.H.P. made by North Eastern Marine Engineering Co. Ltd., Newcastle, double reduction geared to a single screw shaft.
Fully refrigerated capacity.
19.4.1920: Launched by Short Bros. Ltd., Sunderland (Yard No. 398) for Donaldson South American Line Ltd. (Donaldson Bros. Ltd., managers). *10.1920:* Completed. *27.6.1938:* Managers became Donaldson Bros. & Black Ltd. *1941:* Transferred to Donaldson Line Ltd. *5.1948:* Sold to Hector Whaling Ltd., London for service as a storeship and renamed BRANSFIELD, (Bugge & Krohn-Hansen subsequently became managers). *7.1958:* Sold to Eckhardt & Co. K.G., Hamburg. *19.7.1958:* Arrived at Hamburg for demolition.

CORINALDO
National Maritime Museum

62. CORINALDO (I) (1921-1942) Steel steamship.
ON. 144248. 7,131g, 4,417n. 414.5 × 55.6 × 36.7 feet.
Two steam turbines of 736 N.H.P. made by the shipbuilder double reduction geared to a single screw shaft.
Fully refrigerated capacity.
16.8.1920: Launched by Scotts' Shipbuilding & Engineering Co. Ltd., Greenock (Yard No. 482) for Donaldson South American Line Ltd. (Donaldson Bros. Ltd., managers). *2.1921:* Completed. *27.6.1938:* Managers became Donaldson Bros. & Black Ltd. *1941:* Transferred to Donaldson Line Ltd. *29.10.1942:* When on passage from Buenos Aires to Glasgow via Freetown with a cargo of frozen meat she was struck by a torpedo from the German submarine U509. Two further attempts were made to sink her by U659 but in the end she was sunk *30.10.1942* by gunfire and a torpedo by U203 in position 33.20N 18.12W. Seven members of her crew and one gunner were lost.

CORTONA
J. Clarkson

63. CORTONA (I) (1921-1942) Steel steamship.
ON. 144237. 7,093g, 4,453n. 414.4 × 55.7 × 36.8 feet.
Two steam turbines of 729 N.H.P. made by the shipbuilder double reduction geared to a single screw shaft.
Fully refrigerated capacity.
14.8.1920: Launched by Vickers Ltd., Barrow (Yard No. 571) for Donaldson South American Line Ltd. (Donaldson Bros. Ltd., managers). *3.1921:* Completed. *27.6.1938:* Managers became Donaldson Bros. & Black Ltd. *1941:* Transferred to Donaldson Line Ltd. *11.7.1942:* When on passage from Liverpool to Buenos Aires, with a general cargo, she was struck by torpedoes from the German submarines U116 and U201. She remained afloat for some time until U201 administered the *"Coup de grâce"* and sank her in a position 32.45N 24.45W. Thirty members of her crew and two gunners were lost.

NOTE: The reader will now have noticed that the CORRIENTES (I), CORINALDO (I) and the CORTONA (I) proved to be difficult ships to sink, this being entirely due to the large volume of cork insulation fitted in the refrigerated holds of these vessels. The increased inflow of water from the additional damage caused by further attacks eventually overcame the buoyancy properties of the cork.

GRACIA   J. Clarkson

64. GRACIA (I) (1921-1941) Steel steamship.
ON. 144258. 5,642g, 3,537n. 415.5 × 54.2 × 30.8 feet.
Two steam turbines of 736 N.H.P. made by the shipbuilder double reduction geared to a single screw shaft.
Part refrigerated capacity.
6.5.1921: Launched by Scotts' Shipbuilding & Engineering Co. Ltd., Greenock (Yard No. 510) for Donaldson Line Ltd. (Donaldson Bros. Ltd., managers). *6.1921:* Completed. *27.6.1938:* Managers became Donaldson Brothers & Black Ltd. *30.12.1938:* Transferred to Donaldson South American Line Ltd. (Donaldson Bros. & Black Ltd., managers). *19.2.1941:* Bombed and sunk in a position 59.39N 07.24W by German aircraft when on passage from Manchester to St. John N.B. in ballast. All her crew were saved.

ATHENIA   J. Clarkson

65. ATHENIA (II) (1923-1939) Steel steamship.
ON. 146330. 13,465g, 8,118n. 526.3 × 66.4 × 38.1 feet.
Six steam turbines of 8,700 I.H.P. made by the shipbuilder double reduction geared to twin screw shafts.
Part refrigerated capacity.
Originally ordered by Cunard Steam-Ship Co. Ltd. *28.1.1922:* Launched by Fairfield Shipbuilding & Engineering Co. Ltd., Glasgow (Yard No. 596) for Anchor-Donaldson Ltd. (Donaldson Bros. Ltd., managers). *4.1923:* Completed. *1928:* Donaldson Bros. Ltd. and Anchor Line (Henderson Bros.) Ltd., became joint managers. *1935:* Transferred to Donaldson Atlantic Line Ltd. (Donaldson Bros. Ltd., managers). *27.6.1938:* Managers became Donaldson Bros. & Black Ltd. *3.9.1939:* When on passage from Liverpool to Montreal, this being the first day of the Second World War, she was attacked by the German submarine U30 and torpedoed in position 56.44N 14.05W. She sank the following day. Ninety three passengers and 19 crew were lost in the attack and during the abandoning of the vessel.

CORACERO   W.S.S. Brownell collection

66. CORACERO (1923-1943) Steel steamship.
ON. 147852. 7,252g, 4,533n. 423.6 × 56.0 × 36.7 feet.
Triple expansion 3-cyl. steam engine engine of 708 N.H.P. made by J. G. Kincaid & Co. Ltd., Greenock. Some years later an exhaust turbine driving a steam compressor was fitted.
Fully refrigerated capacity.
8.3.1923: Launched by Lithgows Ltd., Port Glasgow (Yard No. 732) for "Coracero" Steamship Co. Ltd. (Donaldson Bros. Ltd. and J. Black & Co. Ltd., managers). *5.1923:* Completed. *1927:* Transferred to Donaldson South American Line Ltd. (Donaldson Bros. Ltd., managers). *27.6.1938:* Managers became Donaldson Bros. & Black Ltd. *1941:* Transferred to Donaldson Line Ltd. *17.3.1943:* When on passage from Buenos Aires and New York to Liverpool with refrigerated cargo, was torpedoed and sunk by the German submarine U384 in a position 51.04N 33.20W. Five members of the crew were lost.

GERALDINE MARY   *Alex Duncan*

67. GERALDINE MARY (1924-1940) Steel steamship.
ON. 151629. 7,244g, 4,595n. 425.1 × 56.1 × 28.5 feet.
Triple expansion 3-cyl. steam engine of 724 N.H.P. made by the shipbuilder.
19.8.1924: Launched by Vickers Ltd., Barrow (Yard No. 605) for Anglo-Newfoundland Development Co. Ltd. (Donaldson Bros. Ltd., managers). *10.1924:* Completed. *1930:* Transferred to Anglo-Newfoundland Steamship Co. Ltd. (Donaldson Bros. Ltd., managers). *27.6.1938:* Managers became Donaldson Bros. & Black Ltd. *4.8.1940:* Torpedoed and sunk by the German submarine U52 in a position 56.46N 15.48W when on passage from Botwood N.F. to Manchester with a cargo of newsprint and paper pulp. Two members of her crew and one passenger were lost.

MOVERIA
                  F. W. Hawks

68. MOVERIA (1925-1952) Steel motor vessel.
ON. 147941. 4,867g, 2,873n. 385.6 × 51.6 × 28.6 feet.
8-cyl. four stroke cycle single acting oil engine of 699 N.H.P. made by the shipbuilder.
Part refrigerated capacity.
10.10.1924: Launched by Vickers Ltd., Barrow (Yard No. 606) for Donaldson Line Ltd. (Donaldson Bros. Ltd., managers). *1.1925:* Completed. *27.6.1938:* Managers became Donaldson Bros. & Black Ltd. *1951:* Owners became Donaldson Atlantic Line Ltd. *6.1952:* Sold to British Iron & Steel Corporation (Salvage) Ltd., for £65,000 for scrapping and allocated to T. W. Ward Ltd. *11.6.1952:* Arrived at Briton Ferry, South Wales, to be broken up.

LETITIA   *Alex Duncan*

69. LETITIA (II) (1925-1946) Steel steamship.
ON. 148847. 13,475g, 8,161n. 525.7 × 66.4 × 29.5 feet.
Six steam turbines of 8700 I.H.P. made by the shipbuilder, double reduction geared to twin screw shafts.
Part refrigerated capacity.
14.10.1924: Launched by Fairfield Shipbuilding & Engineering Co. Ltd., Glasgow (Yard No. 601) for Anchor-Donaldson Ltd. (Donaldson Bros. Ltd. and Anchor Line (Henderson

Bros.) Ltd., joint managers). *4.1925:* Completed. *1935:* Transferred to Donaldson Atlantic Line Ltd. (Donaldson Bros. Ltd., managers). *27.6.1938:* Managers became Donaldson Bros. & Black Ltd. *4.9.1946:* Sold to the Ministry of Transport (Donaldson Bros. & Black Ltd., managers) and renamed EMPIRE BRENT. Used as a troopship between the Far East and the U.K., a "war-bride" ship to North America and an immigrant ship for the Australian Government. *2.1952:* After an extensive refit by Barclay, Curle & Co. Ltd., Glasgow, she was chartered by the New Zealand Government for the immigrant service to Wellington. The terms of the charter were agreed between the British Government and the New Zealand Government allowing the charterer to purchase the vessel on instalments which were part of the charter payments. She was renamed CAPTAIN COOK for the New Zealand service, but remained under the management of Donaldson Bros. & Black Ltd. *1958:* Owners name restyled to Ministry of Transport and Civil Aviation. *10.2.1960:* Taken off service on arrival at Glasgow from the Far East. *1.3.1960:* Arrived to lay-up in the River Fal where she was sold to British Iron & Steel Corporation (Salvage) Ltd. for £182,375 for scrapping and allocated to T. W. Ward Ltd. *29.4.1960:* Arrived at Inverkeithing to be broken up.

CAPTAIN COOK in black livery in the early 1950's   *Skyfotos*

CAPTAIN COOK: The Lounge

CAPTAIN COOK: The Forward Dining Room

CAPTAIN COOK: The Corridor Lounge — probably the same area shown on page 33

CAPTAIN COOK in her subsequent white livery

G. E. Langmuir

75

MODAVIA   *J. Clarkson*

70. MODAVIA (1927-1943) Steel motor vessel.
ON. 148922. 4,858g, 2,859n. 387.0 × 53.7 × 27.5 feet.
8-cyl. four stroke cycle single acting oil engine of 699 N.H.P. made by the shipbuilder. Part refrigerated capacity.
23.9.1926: Launched by Vickers Ltd., Barrow (Yard No. 626) for Donaldson Line Ltd. (Donaldson Bros. Ltd., managers). *4.1927:* Completed. *27.6.1938:* Managers became Donaldson Bros. & Black Ltd. *27.2.1943:* Torpedoed and sunk by a German E-boat in Lyme Bay, 090° 14 miles from Berry Head while on a voyage from Halifax N.S. to Southampton via Milford Haven with general cargo including aluminium. All hands were saved.

VARDULIA   *Alex Duncan*

71. VARDULIA (1929-1935) Steel steamship.
ON. 137835. 5,691g, 3,613n. 423.3 × 56.0 × 28.7 feet.
Triple expansion 3-cyl. steam engine of 564 N.H.P. made by Rankin & Blackmore, Greenock.
1.1917: Launched by Russell and Co., Port Glasgow (Yard No. 691) as VERDUN for Verdun Steamship Co. Ltd. (Gow, Harrison & Co., managers), Glasgow. *3.1917:* Completed. *6.1919:* Sold to Cunard Steam-Ship Co. Ltd., Liverpool and renamed VARDULIA. *2.1929:* Bought by Donaldson Line Ltd. (Donaldson Bros. Ltd., managers). *19/20.10.1935:* When on passage from Hartlepool to Botwood, N.F., she foundered in a position 58.00N 18.30W after developing a severe list during heavy weather. An extensive search of the area revealed nothing of the crew or the ship; all hands perished. She was carrying a cargo of coal.

AIRTHRIA   W.S.P.L.

72. AIRTHRIA (1929-1938) Steel steamship.
ON. 144396. 4,770g, 2,937n. 396.5 × 54.8 × 26.2 feet.
Triple expansion 3-cyl. steam engine of 620 N.H.P. made by the shipbuilder.
17.4.1914: Launched by Flensburger Schiffsbau-Gesellschaft, Flensburg, Germany (Yard No. 338), as LÜBECK for Deutsch-Australische Dampfschiffs-Gesellschaft, Germany. *6.1914:* Completed. *8.1919:* Surrendered as a prize and taken over by The Shipping Controller (British India Steam Navigation Co. Ltd., managers). *18.11.1920:* Sold to The Hain Steamship Co. Ltd., London and renamed TRELEVAN. *3.1929:* Bought by Donaldson Line Ltd. (Donaldson Bros. Ltd., managers) and renamed AIRTHRIA. *2.1938:* Sold to Rederi A/B Atlanta (Birger Krogius, manager) Finland and renamed ANJA. *1941:* Seized by the United States Authorities, taken over by the United States Maritime Commission and operated by the American-West Africa Line Inc., under the Panamanian flag. Renamed SCAPA FLOW. *14.11.1942:* Torpedoed and sunk by the German submarine U134 south west of the Cape Verde Islands in a position 12.00N 30.00W whilst on a voyage from West African ports to Baltimore U.S.A. with a cargo of manganese ore, rubber and latex in drums. Thirty three of her crew were lost.

GREGALIA   *Alex Duncan*

73. GREGALIA (1929-1941) Steel steamship.
ON. 160261. 5,802g, 3,580n. 425.0 × 56.0 × 28.7 feet.
Quadruple expansion 4-cyl. steam engine of 708 N.H.P. made by D. Rowan & Co. Ltd., Glasgow.
Part refrigerated capacity.
27.5.1929: Launched by Lithgows Ltd., Port Glasgow (Yard No. 824) for Donaldson Line Ltd. (Donaldson Bros. Ltd., managers). *7.1929:* Completed. *27.6.1938:* Managers became Donaldson Bros. & Black Ltd. *9.5.1941:* Torpedoed and sunk by the German submarine U201 east of Cape Farewell in a position 60.24N 32.37W. She was sailing in Convoy OB 318 from Glasgow to Buenos Aires in ballast. All hands were saved.

SULAIRIA   *National Maritime Museum*

74. SULAIRIA (1929-1940) Steel steamship.
ON. 161888. 5,802g, 3,580n. 425.0 × 56.0 × 28.7 feet.
Quadruple expansion 4-cyl. steam engine of 708 N.H.P. made by D. Rowan & Co. Ltd., Glasgow.
Part refrigerated capacity.
8.8.1929: Launched by Lithgows Ltd., Port Glasgow (Yard No. 825) for Donaldson Line Ltd. (Donaldson Bros. Ltd., managers). *10.1929:* Completed. *27.6.1938:* Managers became Donaldson Bros. & Black Ltd. *25.9.1940:* Torpedoed and sunk by the German submarine U43 west of Ireland in a position 53.43N 20.10W when on passage from Glasgow to Montreal in Convoy OB 217, from which she had become a "straggler". One member of her crew was lost. She had a cargo of general and livestock.

ESMOND   *National Maritime Museum*

75. ESMOND (1932-1941) Steel steamship.
ON. 161898. 4,976g, 3,131n. 405.3 × 53.4 × 26.1 feet.
Triple expansion 3-cyl. steam engine of 442 N.H.P. made by D. Rowan & Co. Ltd., Glasgow.
27.12.1929: Launched by Charles Connell & Co. Ltd., Glasgow (Yard No. 417) as TRAPRAIN LAW for Law Shipping Co. Ltd. (T. Law & Co., managers) Glasgow. *1.1930:* Completed. *1932:* Bought by Anglo-Newfoundland Steamship Co. Ltd. (Donaldson Bros. Ltd., managers) and renamed ESMOND. *27.6.1938:* Managers became Donaldson Bros. & Black Ltd. *9.5.1941:* Torpedoed and sunk by the German submarine U110 east of Cape Farewell in a position 60.45N 33.02W. She was on passage in ballast from Loch Ewe to Sydney, Cape Breton, N.S. in Convoy OB 318. All hands were saved.

NORTONIAN in Leyland colours　　　　　　　　　　　　　W.S.P.L. Cochrane collection

76. NORTONIAN (1934-1935) Steel steamship.
ON. 135514. 6,367g, 4,097n. 400.7 × 52.4 × 26.9 feet.
Quadruple expansion 4-cyl. steam engine of 507 N.H.P. made by the shipbuilder.
1.10.1913: Launched by D. & W. Henderson & Co. Ltd., Glasgow (Yard No. 485) as NORTONIAN for F. Leyland & Co. Ltd., Liverpool. *11.1913:* Completed. *4.1934:* Bought by Donaldson Line Ltd. (Donaldson Bros. Ltd., managers). *21.8.1935:* Arrived at Genoa. *10.1935:* Sold to Italian shipbreakers for £10,550 and broken up.

NORWEGIAN　　　　　　　　　　　　　　　　　　　　　　J. Clarkson

77. NORWEGIAN (1934-1954) Steel steamship.
ON. 145849. 6,366g, 4,008n. 400.2 × 52.4 × 35.0 feet.
Quadruple expansion 4-cyl. steam engine of 644 N.H.P. made by the shipbuilder.
28.12.1920: Launched by Caledon Shipbuilding & Engineering Co. Ltd., Dundee (Yard No. 254) as NORWEGIAN for F. Leyland & Co. Ltd., Liverpool. *8.1921:* Completed. *7.1934:* Bought by Donaldson Line Ltd. (Donaldson Bros. Ltd., managers). *27.6.1938:* Managers became Donaldson Bros. & Black Ltd. *9.1946:* Transferred to Donaldson Atlantic Line Ltd. (Donaldson Bros. & Black Ltd., managers). *1.1954:* Sold to Cia. de Navegacion Almirante S.A., Panama and renamed MARIA ELAINE. *11.1959:* Sold to Japanese shipbreakers and arrived at Osaka *30.12.1959* to be broken up.

DAKOTIAN *W.S.P.L.*

78. DAKOTIAN (1934-1940) Steel steamship.
ON. 145910. 6,426g, 4,065n. 400.4 × 52.5 × 35.0 feet.
Quadruple expansion 4-cyl. steam engine of 626 N.H.P. made by the shipbuilder.
25.2.1921: Launched by D. & W. Henderson & Co. Ltd., Glasgow (Yard No. 506) as DAKOTIAN for F. Leyland & Co. Ltd., Liverpool. *1.1922:* Completed. *11.1934:* Bought by Donaldson Line Ltd. (Donaldson Bros. Ltd., managers). *27.6.1938:* Managers became Donaldson Bros. & Black Ltd. *21.11.1940:* Mined and sunk in Dale Roads, Milford Haven, during a voyage from Swansea to St. John, N.B. with general cargo and tinplate. The wreck lies in a position 090° five cables from Dale Point.

NUBIAN in Leyland colours *F. W. Hawks*

79. NUBIAN (1934-1935) Steel steamship.
ON. 131431. 6,384g, 4,067n. 400.3 × 52.5 × 35.0 feet.
Quadruple expansion 4-cyl. steam engine of 518 N.H.P. made by North Eastern Marine Engineering Co. Ltd., Newcastle-upon-Tyne.
20.2.1912: Launched by R. & W. Hawthorn, Leslie & Co. Ltd., Newcastle upon Tyne (Yard No. 451) as NUBIAN for F. Leyland & Co. Ltd., Liverpool. *4.1912:* Completed. *11.1934:* Bought by Donaldson Line Ltd. (Donaldson Bros. Ltd., managers). *7.1935:* Sold for £10,750 to Cressdene Shipping Co. Ltd. (Dene Ship Management Co. Ltd., managers) London and resold, under the provisions of the British Shipping (Assistance) Act 1935 for £10,750 to Societa Italiana Ernesto Breda, Marghera, for scrapping. *8.1935:* Arrived in Italy to be broken up.

80. DELILIAN (1936-1954) Steel steamship.
ON. 147207. 6,423g, 4,064n. 400.4 × 52.5 × 35.0 feet.
Quadruple expansion 4-cyl. steam engine of 626 N.H.P. made by the shipbuilder.
16.2.1923: Launched by D. & W. Henderson & Co. Ltd., Glasgow (Yard No. 512) as DELILIAN for F. Leyland & Co. Ltd., Liverpool. *4.1923:* Completed. *4.1934:* Sold

DELILIAN *W.S.S. Brownell collection*

to Charente Steamship Co. Ltd. (T. & J. Harrison, managers) Liverpool. *5.1936:* Bought for £17,500 by Donaldson Line Ltd. (Donaldson Bros. Ltd., managers). *27.6.1938:* Managers became Donaldson Bros. & Black Ltd. *7.3.1941:* When bound for St. John N.B. from the Clyde she was struck by a torpedo on her starboard bow causing extensive damage to the hull in the way of the chain lockers, forepeak tank and No. 1 hold. She was released from convoy and when brought about proceeded east to the Clyde where she eventually arrived safely in Rothesay Bay. She was later repaired and returned to service. *2.1954:* Sold to British Iron & Steel Corporation (Salvage) Ltd. for £44,000 for scrapping and allocated to Smith & Houston Limited. *2.2.1954:* Arrived at Port Glasgow to be broken up.

DORELIAN *J. Clarkson*

81. DORELIAN (1936-1954) Steel steamship.
ON. 147212. 6,431g, 4,069n. 400.4 × 52.4 × 35.0 feet.
Quadruple expansion 4-cyl. steam engine of 626 N.H.P. made by the shipbuilder. *4.4.1923:* Launched by D. & W. Henderson & Co. Ltd., Glasgow (Yard No. 627) as DORELIAN for F. Leyland & Co. Ltd., Liverpool. *5.1923:* Completed. *12.1933:* Sold to Charente Steamship Co. Ltd. (T. & J. Harrison, managers) Liverpool. *9.1936:* Bought by Donaldson Line Ltd. (Donaldson Bros. Ltd., managers). *27.6.1938:* Managers became Donaldson Bros. & Black Ltd. *2.1954:* Sold to British Iron & Steel Corporation (Salvage) Ltd. for £44,000 for scrapping and allocated to W. H. Arnott, Young & Co. Ltd., Dalmuir.

SALACIA, as built, with short funnel   W.S.S. Brownell collection

82. SALACIA (III) (1937-1960) Steel motor vessel.
ON. 165910. 5,495g, 3,286n. 430.6 × 57.2 × 28.1 feet.
5-cyl. two stroke cycle double acting oil engine of 1,025 N.H.P. made by the shipbuilder.
11.3.1937: Launched by Harland & Wolff Ltd., Govan (Yard No. 982G) for Donaldson Line Ltd. (Donaldson Bros. Ltd., managers). *8.1937:* Completed. *27.6.1938:* Managers became Donaldson Bros. & Black Ltd. *3.1960:* Sold to British Iron & Steel Corporation (Salvage) Ltd. for £64,500 for scrapping and allocated to W. H. Arnott, Young & Co. Ltd. *20.3.1960:* Arrived at Dalmuir to be broken up.

SALACIA, with lengthened funnel   W.S.P.L.

83. ROTHERMERE (1938-1941) Steel steamship.
ON. 172631. 5,356g, 3,070n. 421.2 × 56.5 × 25.7 feet.
Quadruple expansion 4-cyl. steam engine of 489 N.H.P. made by D. Rowan & Co. Ltd., Glasgow.
10.11.1938: Launched by Charles Connell & Co. Ltd., Glasgow (Yard No. 424) for Anglo-Newfoundland Steamship Co. Ltd. (Donaldson Bros. & Black Ltd., managers). *12.1938:* Completed. *20.5.1941:* Torpedoed and sunk by the German submarine U98 in position 57.48N 41.36W when on passage from Botwood N.F. to London with a cargo of newsprint and paper pulp. Twenty two lives were lost in the attack.

ROTHERMERE in the Manchester Ship Canal *W.S.S. Brownell collection*

84. CORRIENTES (II) (1946-1954) Steel steamship.
ON. 180133. 7,058g, 4,756n. 431.0 × 56.3 × 35.2 feet.
Triple expansion 3-cyl. steam engine of 537 N.H.P. made by North Eastern Marine Engineering Co. (1938) Ltd., Newcastle-upon-Tyne.
Part refrigerated capacity.
24.12.1943: Launched by Short Bros. Ltd., Sunderland (Yard No. 480) as EMPIRE CROMER for the Ministry of War Transport (Blue Star Line Ltd., managers). *4.1944:* Completed. *20.3.1946:* Bought by Donaldson Line Ltd. (Donaldson Bros. & Black Ltd., managers) and renamed CORRIENTES. *3.1954:* Sold to Blue Star Line Ltd., London who originally proposed to name her OAKLAND STAR but did not proceed with the alteration. *1.1955:* Sold to Williamson & Co. Ltd., Hong Kong and renamed INCHMAY. *1966:* Sold to National Shipping Corporation, Pakistan and renamed KAUKHALI. *2.4.1968:* Arrived at Karachi and laid up. *10.1968:* Sold to Eastern Steel Co., who commenced demolition work at Karachi in *5.1969.*

CORRIENTES *Alex Duncan*

CARMIA

W.S.S. Brownell collection

85. CARMIA (II) (1946-1954) Steel steamship.
ON. 169169. 7,048g, 4,881n. 430.9 × 56.2 × 35.2 feet.
Triple expansion 3-cyl. steam engine of 452 N.H.P. made by North Eastern Marine Engineering Co. (1938) Ltd., Newcastle-upon-Tyne.
Part refrigerated capacity.
2.6.1943: Launched by Armstrong Whitworth & Co. (Shipbuilders) Ltd., Newcastle upon Tyne (Yard No. 4) as EMPIRE FLAG for the Ministry of War Transport (New Zealand Shipping Co. Ltd., managers). *10.1943:* Completed. *16.4.1946:* Bought by Donaldson Line Ltd. (Donaldson Bros. & Black Ltd., managers) and renamed CARMIA. *1946:* Transferred to Donaldson Atlantic Line Ltd. *1949:* Transferred to Donaldson Line Ltd. Management remained Donaldson Bros. & Black Ltd. throughout the transfers.
3.1954: Sold to Blue Star Line Ltd., London and renamed VICTORIA STAR. *10.1955:* Sold to Douglas Steamship Co. Ltd. (Douglas Lapraik & Co., managers) Hong Kong and renamed INCHEARN. *1966:* Sold to Japanese shipbreakers. *26.3.1966:* Arrived at Osaka. *5.1966:* Demolition commenced at Izumi-Ohtsu.

GRACIA

W.S.S. Brownell collection

86. **GRACIA (II) (1946-1954)** Steel steamship.
ON. 168992. 7,040g, 4,973n. 432.7 × 56.2 × 34.2 feet.
Triple expansion 3-cyl. steam engine of 558 N.H.P. made by J. G. Kincaid & Co. Ltd., Greenock.
Part refrigerated capacity.
28.12.1942: Launched by Lithgows Ltd., Port Glasgow (Yard No. 977) as EMPIRE TREASURE for the Ministry of War Transport (Port Line Ltd., managers). *3.1943:* Completed. *10.5.1946:* Bought by Donaldson Line Ltd. (Donaldson Bros. & Black Ltd., managers) and renamed GRACIA. *3.1954:* Sold to Blue Star Line Ltd., London and renamed OREGON STAR. *5.1955:* Sold to Williamson & Co. Ltd., Hong Kong and renamed INCHLEANA. *3.1966:* Sold to National Shipping Corporation, Pakistan and renamed TETULIA. *21.7.1968:* Arrived at Chittagong for service as a barge. *1969:* Broken up at Chittagong by Mohamadi Iron Traders.

PARTHENIA *Alex Duncan*

87. **PARTHENIA (III) (1946-1949)** Steel steamship.
ON. 168201. 6,219g, 3,836n. 397.4 × 55.0 × 31.4 feet.
Steam turbine of 619 N.H.P. made by General Electric Company, Schenectady, New York, U.S.A., double reduction geared to a single screw shaft.
12.1918: Launched by Federal Shipbuilding Company, Kearny, N.J., U.S.A. (Yard No. 4) as MERCER for the United States Shipping Board. *1.1919:* Completed. *1936:* Owners became the United States Maritime Commission. *11.1.1941:* Bought by the Ministry of War Transport and renamed EMPIRE KANGAROO. Donaldson Bros. & Black Ltd., appointed managers. *8.8.1946:* Bought by Donaldson Atlantic Line Ltd. (Donaldson Bros. & Black Ltd., managers) and renamed PARTHENIA. *7.1949:* Sold to Pasquale Mazzella, Italy and renamed ERMINIA MAZZELLA. *1951:* Sold to Achille Onorato fu Vincenzo, Italy and renamed PINA ONORATO. *1958:* Sold to Cantieri Ital Nav, La Spezia and *22.9.1958* arrived at Spezia for demolition.

PARTHENIA lying in Princes Dock, Glasgow, 23.7.1949 just before her sale *E. J. Wylie*

85

LAKONIA   W.S.S. Brownell collection

88. LAKONIA (II) (1947-1962) Steel steamship.
ON. 169915. 7,227g, 4,420n. 441.6 × 57.1 × 34.8 feet.
Triple expansion 3-cyl. steam engine of 668 N.H.P. made by Worthington Pump and Machinery Corporation, Harrison, New Jersey, U.S.A.
10.4.1944: Launched by Bethlehem-Fairfield Shipyard Inc., Baltimore, Maryland, U.S.A. (Yard No. 2351) as SAMTRUSTY for the United States War Shipping Administration. *4.1944:* Completed and bareboat chartered to the Ministry of War Transport (Donaldson Bros. & Black Ltd., managers). *16.4.1947:* Bought by Donaldson Line Ltd., (Donaldson Bros. & Black Ltd., managers) and renamed LAKONIA. *1962:* Sold to Cia. de Nav. "Somerset" S.A., Liberia and renamed SANGAETANO. *2.5.1972:* Arrived at Blyth to be broken up by Hughes Bolckow Ltd.

CORTONA   Roger Sherlock

89. CORTONA (II) (1947-1967) Steel steamship.
ON. 182076. 8,289g, 4,919n. 448' 0" × 62' 9" × 36' 2".
Two steam turbines of 1,579 N.H.P. made by the shipbuilder, double reduction geared to a single screw shaft.
Completely refrigerated capacity.
7.3.1947: Launched by Hawthorn, Leslie & Co. Ltd., Newcastle-upon-Tyne (Yard No. 687) for Donaldson Line Ltd. (Donaldson Bros. & Black Ltd., managers). *9.1947:* Completed. *2.1967:* Sold to Jade Co. Inc., Greece and renamed KAROS. *29.5.1978:* Laid up at Piraeus. *6.1980:* Sold to Taiwan shipbreakers. *25.7.1980:* Nan Long Steel & Iron Co. Ltd. commenced demolition at Kaohsiung where she had arrived prior to *7.7.1980.*

90. LAURENTIA (1947-1966) Steel steamship.
ON. 180899. 8,349g, 4,276n. 455' 2" × 62' 2" × 34' 6".
Two steam turbines of 6,600 S.H.P. made by Westinghouse Electric & Manufacturing Company, Pittsburgh, Pennsylvania, U.S.A., double reduction geared to a single screw shaft.
Limited refrigerated capacity.
10.2.1945: Launched by Permanente Metals Corporation, Shipbuilding Division, Shipyard No. 1, Richmond, California, U.S.A. (Yard No. 586) as the transport MEDINA VICTORY for the United States War Shipping Administration. *3.1945:* Completed. *6.1946:* Chartered by the Ministry of Transport, for service as a troopship, transferred to British registry and managed by Donaldson Bros. & Black Ltd. *29.8.1947:* Sold to the Ministry of Transport. *22.9.1947:* Bought by Donaldson Atlantic Line Ltd. (Donaldson Bros. & Black Ltd., managers) and renamed LAURENTIA. She was refitted by Barclay, Curle & Co. Ltd., Glasgow, as a general cargo vessel with accommodation

LAURENTIA *Alex Duncan*

for 12 passengers. *1948/49:* Extensive reconstruction of accommodation carried out to provide facilities for the carriage of 55 passengers. *1954:* Transferred to the Donaldson Line Ltd. *12.1966:* Sold to Spanish shipbreakers. *4.1.1967:* Arrived at Valencia for demolition.

NOTE: This was the first American merchant vessel to have radar fitted and she carried specially trained U.S. Army personnel to operate the system.

LISMORIA *Alex Duncan*

91. LISMORIA (1948-1967) Steel steamship.
ON. 180910. 8,323g, 4,673n. 455' 2" × 62' 2" × 34' 6".
Two steam turbines of 6,600 S.H.P. made by General Electric Company, Lynn, Massachusetts, U.S.A., double reduction geared to a single screw shaft.
Limited refrigerated capacity.
29.12.1944: Launched by California Shipbuilding Corporation, Los Angeles, Cal., U.S.A.(Yard No. V39) as the transport TAOS VICTORY for the United States War Shipping Administration. *2.1945:* Completed. *6.1946:* Chartered by the Ministry of Transport for service as a troopship, transferred to British registry and managed by Furness, Withy & Co. Ltd. *29.8.1947:* Sold to the Ministry of Transport. Furness, Withy & Co. Ltd., remained managers. *30.3.1948:* Bought by Donaldson Atlantic Line Ltd. (Donaldson Bros. & Black Ltd., managers), converted to a passenger and cargo ship with accommodation for 55 passengers and renamed LISMORIA. *1954:* Transferred to Donaldson Line Ltd. *1.1967:* Sold to Astroguarda Cia. Nav. S.A., Greece and renamed NEON. *24.5.1967:* Arrived at Kaohsiung to be broken up.

NOTE: In 1948 it was proposed to rename this vessel "CABOTIA" but LISMORIA was chosen as being more appropriate.

CORINALDO W.S.P.L.

92. CORINALDO (II) (1949-1967) Steel motor ship.
ON. 182108. 8,378g, 4,957n. 474' 6" × 63' 4" × 35' 2".
6-cyl. two stroke cycle single acting oil engine of 1,342 N.H.P. made by Barclay, Curle & Co. Ltd., Glasgow.
Completely refrigerated capacity.
7.7.1948: Launched by Charles Connell & Co. Ltd., Glasgow (Yard No. 458) for Donaldson Line Ltd. (Donaldson Bros. & Black Ltd., managers). *3.1949:* Completed. *4.1967:* Sold to China Navigation Co. Ltd. (John Swire & Sons Ltd., managers), London and renamed NINGPO. *8.1967:* Sold to Criomar Inc., Liberia and renamed KINAROS. *1978:* Transferred to Greek registry. *3.2.1980:* Arrived at Kaohsiung for scrapping from Piraeus where she had been laid up since *24.6.1979*. *25.2.1980:* Sing Cheng Yung Iron & Steel Co. Ltd., commenced demolition work.

CALGARIA *Alex Duncan*

93. CALGARIA (1956-1963) Steel motor vessel.
ON. 168687. 8,418g, 4,817n. 494' 2" × 64' 4" × 29' 11".
Two 4-cyl. two stroke cycle single acting oil engines of 9,000 S.H.P. made by the shipbuilder, driving twin screws.
14.5.1941: Launched by Barclay, Curle & Co. Ltd., Glasgow (Yard No. 680) as EMPIRE PRIDE for the Ministry of War Transport (Bibby Bros. & Co., managers). *9.1941:* Completed. *1946:* Owners restyled as Ministry of Transport. *6.1954:* Sold to Charlton Steam Shipping Co. Ltd. (Chandris (England) Ltd., managers), London and renamed CHARLTON PRIDE. *1.1956:* Bought by Donaldson Line Ltd. (Donaldson Bros. & Black Ltd., managers) and renamed CALGARIA. *4.1963:* Sold to Fortaleza Cia. Nav. S.A., Greece and renamed EMBASSY. *6.1963:* Sold for scrapping at Hong Kong. She had loaded a full cargo of scrap at Liverpool and arrived at Hong Kong *9.7.1963* via Cuba.

SANTONA, as built   Alex Duncan

94. SANTONA (II) (1959-1967) Steel motor vessel.
ON. 301396. As built: 1,769g, 756n. 294' 6" × 44' 11" × 17' 11".
As rebuilt: 2,151g, 1,068n. 355' 3" × 44' 11" × 17' 8¾".
5-cyl. two stroke cycle single acting oil engine of 2,000 S.H.P. made by British Polar Engines Ltd., Glasgow.
26.5.1959: Launched by Hall, Russell & Co. Ltd., Aberdeen (Yard No. 877) for Donaldson Line Ltd., (Donaldson Bros. & Black Ltd., managers). *7.1959:* Completed. *1966:* Lengthened by the insertion of an additional hold by Barclay, Curle & Co. Ltd., who carried out the work in Elderslie Drydock, Glasgow. *4.1967:* Transferred to Donaldson Line Holdings Ltd., subsequently Donaldson Line Ltd. *7.1974:* Sold to Maldives Shipping Ltd., Maldive Islands and renamed MALDIVE TRADER. *9.1.1983:* Stranded on North Jumna Shoal, South East of Port Sudan in position 19.27N 37.47E. On being refloated and surveyed she was declared a constructive total loss, temporary repairs were carried out and she then proceeded to Karachi. *2.4.1983:* Arrived at Gadani Beach to be broken up by S. M. Sadik.

NOTE: In 1966, during the lengthening operation the vessel was cut in two, made water-tight and ballasted to maintain a suitable trim for flooding the dock prior to the insertion of the additional section of hull. Due to a mis-calculation and on flooding the dock, the forward section fell over onto the edge of the dock causing considerable damage.

SANTONA after being lengthened   Alex Duncan

COLINA, as built   W.S.P.L.

95. COLINA (II) (1960-1967) Steel motor vessel.
ON. 301410. As built: 1,776g, 756n. 294' 6" × 44' 11" × 17' 11".
As rebuilt: 2,222g, 1,054n. 355' 3" × 44' 11" × 17' 8¾".
5-cyl. two stroke cycle single acting oil engine of 2,000 S.H.P. made by British Polar Engines Ltd., Glasgow.
1.2.1960: Launched by Hall, Russell & Co. Ltd., Aberdeen (Yard No. 878) for Donaldson Line Ltd. (Donaldson Bros. & Black Ltd., managers). *4.1960:* Completed. *1966:* Lengthened by the insertion of an additional hold by Barclay, Curle & Co. Ltd., who carried out the work in Elderslie Drydock, Glasgow. *5.1967:* Sold to Chimo Shipping Ltd., St. Johns, N.F., Canada and renamed ANDREW C. CROSBIE. *1977:* Sold to Carrick Marine Enterprises Corporation, Greece and renamed AKTIAN. *1982:* Arrested by the Cuban Authorities for the non-payment of outstanding accounts. Auctioned and taken over by Empresa de Nav. Mambisa, Cuba. *12.1987:* Reported scrapped at Bahia Honda, 60 miles west of Havana, Cuba.

NOTE: In January 1963, a chartered trip, the COLINA was on passage from Port Talbot and Liverpool to Haifa via Gibraltar. When struck by severe weather off North Africa she developed a heavy list due to leaking oil containers which in turn caused pallets of tinplate to shift. Fortunately she managed to reach the Sardinian port of Cagliari, where the remains of tinplate and oil consignments were resecured and the passage resumed.

COLINA, after lengthening and in Chimo Lines colours   *Alex Duncan*

LETITIA   *Alex Duncan*

96. LETITIA (III) (1961-1967) Steel motor vessel.
ON. 301443. 4,667g, 2,468n. 416' 3" × 58' 2" × 23' 7".
6-cyl. two stroke cycle single acting oil engine of 5,400 S.H.P. made by Sulzer Bros. Ltd., Winterthur, Switzerland.
Limited refrigerated capacity.
16.1.1961: Launched by Hall, Russell & Co. Ltd., Aberdeen (Yard No. 890) for Donaldson Line Ltd. (Donaldson Bros. & Black Ltd., managers). *4.1961:* Completed. *7.1967:* Sold to Wm. Brandts (Leasing) Ltd., London, managed by J. & J. Denholm (Management) Ltd., Glasgow and renamed BIBI. *1976:* Sold to Mercury Ltd. (Denholm Maclay & Co. Ltd., managers) Liberia. *1977:* Sold to Transportacion Maritima Mexicana S.A., Mexico and renamed TEPIC. *1984:* Sold to Wesser de Inversiones S.A., Honduras and renamed TEPORA. *11.3.1985:* Whilst on passage from New Orleans to Vera Cruz, Mexico fire broke out in the cargo spaces when she was about 450 miles south of New Orleans. The crew abandoned ship and were picked up by the U.S.C.G. cutter "DEPENDABLE". The Americans placed a fire-fighting party on board and they extinguished the blaze and connected a tow line. The following day the fire broke out again, the tow was disconnected and on *14.3.1985* she sank about 150 miles north of the Yucatan Peninsula in a position 24.02N 89.00W.

MISCELLANEOUS CRAFT OWNED OR MANAGED BY DONALDSON LINE

The following vessels were owned by Donaldson Line and operated on the Clyde, shipping grain from point to point as required. They were the last mineral barges used on the Forth and Clyde Canal. They were of similar construction to the famous Clyde "Puffers" and had the Donaldson colours on their funnels.

The names used for these vessels were REBECCA, MARY and GARTSHERRIE.

(Left to right) **REBECCA, MARY** and **GARTSHERRIE**   *Scottish Maritime Museum*

The following vessels were owned by the Anglo-Newfoundland Development Company (Donaldson Bros. Ltd., managers) but were operated by Newfoundland shore staff and crews, Donaldson Line staff had no direct involvement.

FLEETWOOD	Wooden Schooner	250 gross	Built 1919
FLEETWAY	Wooden Schooner	250 gross	Built 1919
FLORENCIA	Steel Trawler	290 gross	Built 1917
SORDELLO	Wooden Schooner	582 gross	Built 1919
BELLA SCOTT	Wooden Schooner	504 gross	Built 1918

SHIPS MANAGED ON BEHALF OF H.M. GOVERNMENT
A. WORLD WAR I

A.1 WAR OSTRICH (1918-1919) Steel steamship.
ON. 142609. 5,264g, 3,205n. 400.2 × 52.4 × 28.4 feet.
Triple expansion 3-cyl. steam engine of 517 N.H.P., made by Blair & Co. Ltd., Stockton on Tees.
6.6.1918: Launched by Richardson, Duck & Co. Ltd., Stockton on Tees (Yard No. 672) for The Shipping Controller. *8.1918:* Completed and Donaldson Bros. Ltd., appointed managers. *9.1919:* Sold to Maritime Shipping and Trading Co. Ltd. (G. C. Gibson, manager), London and renamed CUTCOMBE. *8.1928:* Sold to The Ben Line Steamers Limited (W. Thomson and Co., managers), Leith and renamed BENNEVIS. *7.9.1940:* Damaged during an air-raid whilst berthed at London. *9.12.1941:* Captured by Japanese forces off Hong Kong whilst on passage from Hong Kong to Singapore and taken to Hainan Island. Later renamed GYOKUYO MARU. *14.11.1944:* Torpedoed and sunk east of Shanghai by the United States submarine "SPADEFISH" in position 31.04N 123.56E.

A.2 WAR EMU (1918-1919) Steel steamship.
For full details of this vessel, refer to TRITONIA (III) in Fleet List numbered 58.

B. WORLD WAR II

B.1 EMPIRE KANGAROO (1941-1946) Steel steamship.
For full details of this vessel, refer to PARTHENIA (III) in the Fleet List numbered 87.

EMPIRE WHALE as WINONA COUNTY   *W.S.P.L.*

B.2 EMPIRE WHALE (1941-1943) Steel steamship.
ON. 168194. 6,159g, 3,667n. 395.5 × 55.0 × 31.4 feet.
Two steam turbines of 645 N.H.P. by Midwest Engine Company, Indianapolis, Indiana, U.S.A., double reduction geared to a single screw shaft.
16.8.1919: Launched by Federal Shipbuilding Company, Kearny, N.J., U.S.A. (Yard No. 24) as WINONA COUNTY for the United States Shipping Board. *9.1919:* Completed. *1937:* Owners restyled the United States Maritime Commission. *10.1.1941:* Bought by the Ministry of War Transport, renamed EMPIRE WHALE and placed under the management of Donaldson Bros. & Black Ltd. *29.3.1943:* Torpedoed and sunk in the Western Approaches in a position 46.44N 16.38W by the German submarine U662 while sailing in Convoy SL126 from Pepel and Freetown to Methil and the Tyne with a cargo of iron ore. 41 crew, four gunners and one passenger lost their lives.

B.3 EMPIRE CONDOR (1941-1942) Steel steamship.
ON. 168167. 7,773g, 4,586n. 469.0 × 69.6 × 29.2 feet.
Two steam turbines of 1,417 N.H.P. made by De Laval Steam Turbine Co., Trenton, New Jersey, U.S.A., double reduction geared to a single screw shaft.
27.4.1940: Launched by Federal Shipbuilding and Dry Dock Company, Kearny, N.J., U.S.A (Yard No. 165) as the ALMERIA LYKES for the United States Maritime Commission. *7.1940:* Completed and operated by Lykes Bros. S.S. Co. Inc. U.S.A. *21.4.1941:* Transferred on loan to the Ministry of War Transport, renamed EMPIRE CONDOR and placed under the management of Donaldson Bros. & Black Ltd. *13.4.1942:* Returned to the United States Maritime Commission and renamed ALMERIA LYKES. *13.8.1942:* Torpedoed and sunk by E-boats off Cape Bon, Tunisia whilst sailing to Malta in convoy (Operation Pedestal) in position 36.40N 11.35E. The vessel was carrying a full general cargo. The crew of 48, 20 army gunners, 17 U.S. gunners and nine army personnel were all saved.

B.4 EMPIRE CURLEW (1941-1942) Steel steamship.
ON. 168169. 7,101g, 4,258n. 452.5 × '66.2 × 29.4 feet.
Two steam turbines of 1,050 N.H.P. made by the shipbuilder, double reduction geared to a single screw shaft.
7.1940: Launched by Bethlehem Steel Company, Shipbuilding Division, Sparrow's Point, Maryland, U.S.A. (Yard No. 4342) as ROBIN DONCASTER for Seas Shipping Co. Inc., U.S.A. *4.1941:* Completed. *16.4.1941:* Transferred on loan to the Ministry of War Transport, renamed EMPIRE CURLEW and placed under the management of Donaldson Bros. & Black Ltd. *17.4.1942:* Returned to the United States War Shipping Administration and renamed ROBIN DONCASTER. *4.10.1943-4.1.1944:* Converted by Sullivan Drydock Co. Inc., New York into a troopship for the United States Navy, with accommodation provided for 1,756 troops. *4.4.1946:* Reverted to United States Maritime Commission, War Shipping Reserve Fleet. *1948:* Sold to Seas Shipping Co. Inc., U.S.A. *1957:* Sold to Flying Gull Inc., U.S.A. and renamed FLYING GULL. *1961:* Sold to American Export Lines Inc., U.S.A. *1965:* Owners became American Export Isbrandtsen Lines Inc., U.S.A. *1968:* Sold for scrapping to Ferromar Inc., U.S.A. and resold to Eckhardt & Co. G.m.b.H., West Germany who in turn sold her to Hierros Arbulu, Spain. *21.6.1968:* Arrived in tow at Bilbao to be broken up.

B.5 EMPIRE REDSHANK (1941-1943) Steel steamship.
ON. 168170. 6,615g, 4,124n. 395.5 × 55.0 × 31.4 feet.
Steam turbine of 619 N.H.P. by General Electric Company, Schenectady, N.Y., U.S.A., double reduction geared to a single screw shaft.
3.1919: Launched by Federal Shipbuilding Company, Kearny, N.J., U.S.A. (Yard No. 10) as BRADDOCK for the United States Shipping Board. *4.1919:* Completed. *1937:* Owners restyled the United States Maritime Commission. *4.2.1941:* Bought by the Ministry of War Transport, renamed EMPIRE REDSHANK and placed under the management of Donaldson Bros. & Black Ltd. *31.1.1942:* Damaged by air attack when in position 63.24N 02.24W, N.E. of the Faeroes. *22.2.1943:* Torpedoed in mid-Atlantic in position 47.00N 34.30W by the German submarine U606 while sailing in Convoy ON166 from Cardiff and Belfast Lough to Galveston in ballast. Subsequently sunk by gunfire from H.M.S. "TRILLIUM". The crew of 40 and seven gunners were all saved.

B.6 EMPIRE SPRING (1941-1942) Steel motor vessel.
ON. 167002. 6,946g, 4,147n. 432.2 × 56.2 × 34.3 feet.
6-cyl. four stroke cycle single acting oil engine of 490 N.H.P. made by J. G. Kincaid & Co. Ltd., Greenock.
18.3.1941: Launched by Lithgows Ltd., Port Glasgow (Yard No. 944) as EMPIRE SPRING for the Ministry of War Transport (Donaldson Bros. & Black Ltd., managers). *6.1941:* Completed. *14.2.1942:* Torpedoed and sunk by the German submarine U576 in position 42.00N 55.00W (P.A.) whilst sailing in ballast from Manchester to Halifax N.S. 40 of the crew were lost in the attack.

OCEAN WANDERER   W.S.S. Brownell collection

B.7 OCEAN WANDERER (1942-1946) Steel steamship.
ON. 168836. 7,178g, 4,280n. 425.1 × 57.0 × 34.8 feet.
Triple expansion 3-cyl. steam engine of 505 N.H.P. made by General Machinery Corporation, Hamilton, Ohio, U.S.A.
14.6.1942: Launched by Todd-Bath Iron Shipbuilding Corporation, South Portland, Maine, U.S.A. (Yard No. 14) as OCEAN WANDERER for the Ministry of War Transport (Donaldson Bros. & Black Ltd., managers). *7.1942:* Completed. *1946:* Bolton Steam Shipping Co. Ltd., appointed managers. *1.4.1946:* Owners restyled Ministry of Transport. *28.11.1947:* Sold to Bolton Steam Shipping Co. Ltd., London and renamed RUYSDAEL. *1951:* Sold to Kronos Compania Naviera S.A., Costa Rica and renamed SANTA IRENE. *1959:* Transferred to Greek registry. *2.11.1962:* Went aground on Los Cadezos Shoal, four miles west of Tarifa, Spain, during a voyage from Gdansk to Venice with a cargo of coal. *9.11.1962:* Broke in two and became a total loss.

EMPIRE BARDOLPH as MEMLING   W.S.S. Brownell collection

B.8 EMPIRE BARDOLPH (1943-1945) Steel steamship.
ON. 169109. 7,063g, 4,241n. 431.0 × 56.3 × 35.2 feet.
Triple expansion 3-cyl. steam engine of 537 N.H.P. made by North Eastern Marine Engineering Co. (1938) Ltd., Newcastle-upon-Tyne.
8.12.1942: Launched by Short Bros. Ltd., Sunderland as EMPIRE BARDOLPH for the Ministry of War Transport (Donaldson Bros. & Black Ltd., managers). *3.1943:* Completed. *1945:* Management transferred to Lamport & Holt Line Ltd., Liverpool. *10.11.1945:* Sold to Lamport & Holt Line Ltd. *1946:* Renamed MEMLING. *1953:* Sold to Blue Star Line Ltd., London and renamed VANCOUVER STAR. *1957:* Transferred to Lamport & Holt Line Ltd. and renamed MEMLING. *9.1949:* Sold for £44,000 to N.V. Simon's Metaalhandel, Holland for scrapping. *19.10.1959:* Arrived at Rotterdam. *1.2.1960:* Demolition commenced.

EMPIRE PICKWICK as HARINGHATA　　　　　　　　　　*W.S.S. Brownell collection*

B.9 EMPIRE PICKWICK (1943-1946) Steel steamship.
ON. 169053. 7,068g, 4,778n. 430.9 × 56.2 × 35.2 feet.
Triple expansion 3-cyl. steam engine of 542 N.H.P. made by the shipbuilder.
31.8.1943: Launched by J. Readhead & Sons Ltd., South Shields (Yard No. 536) as EMPIRE PICKWICK for the Ministry of War Transport (Donaldson Bros. & Black Ltd., managers). *11.1943:* Completed. *1.4.1946:* Owners restyled the Ministry of Transport. *25.5.1946:* Management transferred to Cayzer, Irvine & Co. Ltd., Glasgow. *31.12.1947:* Sold to The Clan Line Steamers Ltd. (Cayzer, Irvine & Co. Ltd., managers) Glasgow and in *1948* renamed CLAN MACKENDRICK. *1961:* Sold to Mullion & Co. Ltd., Hong Kong and renamed ARDPATRICK. *1966:* Sold to National Shipping Corporation, Pakistan and renamed HARINGHATA. *16.7.1968:* Arrived at Karachi to be broken up.

EMPIRE ARQUEBUS as AL SUDAN　　　　　　　　　*Table Bay Underway Shipping*

B.10 EMPIRE ARQUEBUS (1944, 1945-1946) Steel steamship.
ON. 169819. 7,177g, 4,823n. 396.5 × 60.1 × 35.0 feet.
Two steam turbines made by Westinghouse Electric & Manufacturing Company, Essington, Pennsylvania, U.S.A., double reduction geared to a single screw shaft.
16.11.1943: Launched by Consolidated Steel Corporation Ltd., Wilmington, California, U.S.A. (Yard No. 355) as CAPE ST. VINCENT for the United States War Shipping Administration. Transferred on bareboat charter to the Ministry of War Transport and

completed in *1.1944* as the EMPIRE ARQUEBUS. Placed under the management of Donaldson Bros. & Black Ltd. *1944:* Taken over by the Royal Navy, converted into an Infantry Landing Ship (L.S.I.) and in *1.1945* renamed CICERO (F170). *9.1945:* Returned to the Ministry of War Transport and the management of Donaldson Bros. & Black Ltd. and renamed EMPIRE ARQUEBUS. *1.4.1946:* Charterers restyled the Ministry of Transport. *1946:* Returned to the United States War Shipping Administration and resold to Societe Misr de Navigation Maritime S.A.E. Egypt, renamed AL SUDAN and converted to a passenger ship with accommodation provided for 58 first, 117 second and 1,255 third class passengers. *1961:* Owners became United Arab Maritime Co., United Arab Republic. *1973:* Owners became the Egyptian Navigation Co., Egypt. *1980:* Sold to Rekabie Mousa el Souger, Egypt and arrived at Suez *20.10.1980* for breaking up. *7.1984:* Work reported not yet started.

B.11 SAMHORN (1944-1948) Steel steamship.
ON. 169833. 7,253g, 4,373n. 422.8 × 57.0 × 34.8 feet.
Triple expansion 3-cyl. steam engine made by the Vulcan Iron-Works, Wilkes-Barre, Pennsylvania, U.S.A.
4.2.1944: Launched by Southeastern Shipbuilding Corporation, Savannah, Georgia, U.S.A. (Yard No. 40) as SAMHORN for the United States War Shipping Administration. *2.1944:* Completed and bareboat chartered to the Ministry of War Transport (Donaldson Bros. & Black Ltd., managers). *1.4.1946:* Charterers restyled Ministry of Transport. *3.5.1948:* Returned to the United States Maritime Commission. *1959:* Sold to United States shipbreakers. *8.1.1960:* Demolition commenced at Orange, Texas.

B.12 SAMFINN (1944-1947) Steel steamship.
ON. 169876. 7,255g, 4,372n. 422.8 × 57.0 × 34.8 feet.
Triple expansion 3-cyl. steam engine made by General Machinery Corporation, Hamilton, Ohio, U.S.A.
31.3.1944: Launched by J. A. Jones Construction Company Inc., Brunswick, Georgia, U.S.A. (Yard No. 137) as SAMFINN for the United States War Shipping Administration. *4.1944:* Completed and bareboat chartered to the Ministry of War Transport (Donaldson Bros. & Black Ltd., managers). *1.4.1946:* Charterers restyled Ministry of Transport. *4.9.1947:* Returned to the United States Maritime Commission. *1.1962:* Sold for scrap and demolition commenced at Mobile, Alabama.

B.13 SAMTRUSTY (1944-1947) Steel steamship.
For full details of this vessel, refer to LAKONIA (II) in Fleet List numbered 88.

Appendix 1: THE DONALDSON AND BLACK COMPANIES

Initially, as noted on page 15, Donaldson ships were owned on the 64th share basis but starting in 1899, a number of single ship limited liability companies were incorporated. In 1913 these companies were consolidated into the newly-formed Donaldson Line Ltd.

The various Donaldson companies were as follows:

Glasgow and Newport News S.S. Co. Ltd.
Incorporated: 14.11.1899. Voluntarily liquidated: 30.9.1913.
Capital: £55,000 (£100 shares)

The largest shareholder was Archibald Falconer Donaldson, the next largest being Chesapeake & Ohio Railway Company, Richmond, Virginia.

Parthenia S.S. Co. Ltd.
Incorporated: 14.6.1901. Voluntarily liquidated 30.9.1913.
Capital: £45,000 (£100 shares)

The majority of the shares were held by the Donaldson family. Some shares were held in North America.

Athenia S.S. Co. Ltd.
Incorporated: 23.4.1904. Voluntarily liquidated: 30.9.1913.
Capital: £50,000 (£100 shares)

The major shareholders were A. F. Donaldson and Vickers, Sons & Maxim Ltd.

Cassandra S.S. Co. Ltd.
Incorporated: 22.3.1906. Voluntarily liquidated: 30.9.1913.
Capital: £55,000 (£100 shares)

The major shareholders were the Donaldson family, Glasgow and Newport News S.S. Co. Ltd. and Scotts' Shipbuilding and Engineering Company Ltd., Greenock.

Pythia S.S. Co. Ltd.
Incorporated: 9.12.1909. Voluntarily liquidated: 29.1.1912.
Capital: £2,000 (£1 shares)

Formed following an agreement with Barclay, Curle & Co. Ltd. to own and operate a steamer these builders had taken as part-payment. Barclay, Curle & Co. Ltd. held 1,993 of the shares and the board were all Barclay, Curle men.

Saturnia S.S. Co. Ltd.
Incorporated: 26.3.1910. Voluntarily liquidated: 30.9.1913.
Capital: £52,000 (£100 shares)

The Glasgow & Newport News S.S. Co. Ltd. held 49 shares. Other small holders outside the Donaldson family were Robert Reford and Co., Montreal (25) and the Company insurance broker William Albert St. Aubyn Angove, London (10).

Letitia S.S. Co. Ltd.
Incorporated: 6.3.1912. Voluntarily liquidated: 30.9.1913.
Capital: £80,000 (£100) shares

The majority of the shares were held by the Donaldson family but minority holders were the same as for the Saturnia S.S. Co. Ltd.

Donaldson Brothers Ltd.
Incorporated: 28.2.1913. Voluntarily liquidated: 13.9.1938.
Capital: £200,000 (40,000 £1 Cumulative Preference shares (6%) and 160,000 £1 Ordinary shares).
The majority of the shares were held by the Donaldson family.
27.10.1919: Capital increased to £400,000 by the introduction of 200,000 new £1 Ordinary shares.
1938: Company wound up following the formation of Donaldson Brothers & Black Ltd.

Donaldson Brothers & Black Ltd.
Incorporated: 27.6.1938. Voluntarily liquidated: 20.4.1970.
Capital: £20,000 (16,000 "A" £1 shares and 4,000 "B" £1 shares). Initially all "A" shares were held by the Donaldson family and the "B" shares by the Black family.

Donaldson Line Ltd.
(20.2.1967: Renamed Donaldson Line Holdings Ltd.)
Incorporated: 8.8.1913. Voluntarily liquidated: 23.5.1967.
Capital: £560,000 (£1 shares)
By 3.1914: 552,218 shares had been issued (423,434 in Donaldson hands and 25,920 with Vickers Ltd.).
24.3.1919: Due to appreciation of Capital Assets a distribution of surplus capital in cash was agreed, 10/- for every £1 share held.
27.10.1919: Capital increased to £1,250,000.
18.11.1919: Agreed to distribute excess capital by issue of bonus shares, fully paid up on basis of one for one.
3.1925: Donaldson holding now 840,012 shares of the 1,104,436 shares issued.
28.2.1927: Vickers Ltd. sold their holding to Donaldson.
1938: Donaldson Line Ltd. purchased Donaldson South American Line Ltd. in which shares were held as follows:-

Donaldson Bros. Ltd.	59,852
Vickers Ltd.	89,940
Glasgow Steam Shipping Co. Ltd.	216,346

Glasgow Steam Shipping Co. Ltd. to receive 108,173 Donaldson Line shares for their holding.
4.1940: The Black family held 52,881 each of Cumulative Preference shares and Ordinary shares whilst the Donaldson family held 449,731 Cumulative Preference shares and 456,733 Ordinary shares out of a total of 556,855 each issued.
2.6.1943: Resolution passed to allow investment in air transport.
10.10.1944: Issued Ordinary shares reduced to 4/- each by cash payment of 16/-. Then 445,484 new £1 shares created to maintain £1.25 million total.
22.12.1949: Undivided profits capitalised. £445,484 distributed as 2,227,420 Ordinary shares of 4/- each to shareholders. Then all 4/- shares consolidated into 556,855 £1 Ordinary shares.
29.3.1957: Capital increased to £2 million.
1957: Commenced trading to Great Lakes with chartered tonnage.
1961: Joint service with Cunard Steam-Ship Company Ltd. from Bristol Channel ports to Eastern Canadian ports.
1963: Invested in Caledonian Airways (Prestwick) Ltd.
1964: Purchased White Heather Holidays. Donaldson Line (Air Services) Ltd. incorporated to operate it.

Anchor-Donaldson Ltd.
(10.7.1935: Renamed Donaldson Atlantic Line Ltd.)
Incorporated: 21.11.1916. Voluntarily liquidated: 26.5.1954.
Capital £250,000 (£1 shares)
　The holdings were:

Donaldson Line Ltd. and Donaldson Bros. Ltd.	12,500
Donaldson Line Ltd.	112,497
Anchor Line (Henderson Bros.) Ltd.	125,000

9.8.1923: Capital increased by 250,000 £1 shares of which 200,000 issued at par to Donaldson Bros. Ltd. and Anchor Line (Henderson Bros.) Ltd. on a 50/50 ratio.
1.4.1932: Anchor Line transferred 124,996 shares to Glasgow nominees, Union Bank of Scotland Ltd.
15.3.1935: Anchor Line transferred 35,714 shares to the above nominees and 64,286 to Donaldson Line Ltd.
23.2.1942: Union Bank transferred 76,274 shares to Donaldson Line Ltd. and 84,436 to H.M. Treasury, who also took the last 4 shares held by Anchor Line Ltd., in liquidation.
12.12.1944: H.M. Treasury transferred 84,440 shares to Donaldson Line Ltd. who now held 449,994 shares.

Donaldson South American Line Ltd.
Incorporated: 3.12.1919. Voluntarily liquidated: 21.3.1941.
Capital: £1,000,000 (£1 shares).
　The shareholders were:

Donaldson Line Ltd.	509,997
Glasgow Steam Shipping Co. Ltd.	269,997
Vickers Ltd.	219,999

25.3.1932: Capital reduced to £625,000 by converting £1 shares to 12/6 shares in view of reduced value of assets.
1938: Vickers share-holding acquired by Donaldson Line Ltd.

Coracero S.S. Co. Ltd.
Incorporated: 3.5.1923. Voluntarily liquidated: 16.11.1927.
Capital: £1,000 (£1 shares)
　Lithgows, the builders of the CORACERO held 990 shares, the Donaldson family five and the Black family five. In 1924 the Lithgows holding was transferred to the Donaldson South American Line Ltd.

Donaldson Line Holdings Limited
(24.3.1967: Renamed Donaldson Line Ltd.)
Incorporated: 17.3.1967. Voluntarily liquidated: 27.1.1987.
Capital £430,000 (£1 shares)
　Formed to acquire the trade and name of the Donaldson Line Ltd. and the motor vessel SANTONA (II), then to change name.
　Two shares were issued on formation, then 429,998 shares sold to The Ulster S.S. Co. Ltd.
　Company continued to "further interests of parent company in Scotland."

Another family company operating from Glasgow was the Black family, which would eventually form close ties with the Donaldson Line, initially on the operation of the South American trades including the shipment of meat from the Argentine.

Glasgow Steam Shipping Co. Ltd.
Incorporated: 2.2.1899. Voluntarily liquidated: 4.11.1938.
To acquire in 1899 from John Black & Co. (managers) and 64th holders the steamers KELVIN and KELVINDALE also for the new steamer KELVINGROVE, under construction.***
*** This was a private company. The control and most of the shares being with the Black family.
Capital: £100,000 (4,000 £10 Preference shares and 6,000 Ordinary shares)
5.6.1917: 2,000 un-issued Ordinary shares distributed as paid up bonus, from the Reserve Fund.
11.7.1919: Capital increased to £190,000 by creation of 9,000 new £10 shares. 31.7.1919: These new shares issued as bonus paid-up shares in the ratio of three for every two Ordinary shares held. On liquidation, paid £5 14s. 3d. cash per £10 share held, also pro-rata distribution of 108,162 £1 Ordinary shares and 108,162 £1 5% Preference shares held in the Donaldson Line Ltd.

John Black & Co. Ltd.
Incorporated: 3.6.1919. Voluntarily liquidated: 27.8.1940.
Capital: £50,000 (£10 shares)
Initially all 4,500 shares were held by directors — J. A. Black 2,250, A. A. S. Black 1,350 and A. E. Black 900. In 1933, I. H. S. Black appointed a director, received 600 shares from A. A. S. Black. The same year the last 500 shares were issued to J. A. Black and A. E. Black (150 each) and A. A. S. Black (200).
On liquidation £12,000 Cumulative Preference paid at par, rest of Cumulative Preference shares settled by distribution of 13,224 Donaldson Line £1 shares. Ordinary Shareholders received £8 1s. 4d. per share cash and 1,256 Donaldson Line £1 Preference and 28,257 Ordinary shares.

Single ship companies involved with the Black family:-

Queen Elizabeth Shipping Company Ltd.
Incorporated: 28.3.1890. Voluntarily liquidated: 4.8.1916.
Vessel QUEEN ELIZABETH

Queen Margaret Shipping Company Ltd.
Incorporated: 14.4.1893. Voluntarily liquidated: 10.7.1913.
Vessel: QUEEN MARGARET

Lancefield Steam Shipping Company Ltd.
Incorporated: 23.8.1904. Voluntarily liquidated: 2.12.1912.

Fleet List of John Black & Co., Glasgow
(1919: J. Black & Company Limited)

CHIGNECTO*	BRODICK CASTLE*
PARAGON*	KELVINGROVE (I)
CHARLES CONNELL*	KELVIN (I)†
JESSIE RENWICK*	KELVINDALE †.
QUEEN VICTORIA*	

Note: *Sailing Vessel
†. To Glasgow Steam Shipping Co. Ltd.

Glasgow Steam Shipping Company Ltd. (1899)

KELVIN (I)	KELVIN (II)	KELVINIA (I)
KELVINDALE	KELVINHEAD	KELVINBRAE
KELVINGROVE (II) ‡	CAMBRIAN KING	KELVINBANK (II)
KELVINSIDE	LANCEFIELD	KELVINIA (II)
KELVINBANK (I)		

Note: ‡. 1915 became MERCURIA (Donaldson Line)

Lancefield Steam Shipping Company Ltd.
CAMBRIAN KING †.
FITZCLARENCE

Note: †. To Glasgow Steam Shipping Company Ltd.

Shipping Controller
WAR BREAKER
WAR RIPPLE

Livery used by Glasgow Steam Shipping Company Limited.
Funnel: Buff with black top.
Company flag: Blue with red edge, white letters on blue ground. "G.S.S.Co."

DIVIDEND AND DISTRIBUTION RECORD DURING THE FINAL STAGES OF THE DONALDSON LINE OPERATION

Year	Dividend on Ord. Shares	Additions
1953	10%	15% from reserves
1954	10%	Nil
1955	10%	Nil
1956	15%	Nil
1957	7½%	Scrip Issue (1 for 1)
1958	Nil	Nil
1959	7½%	Nil
1960	2½%	Nil
1961	2½%	Nil
1962	Nil	5% from reserves
1963	2½%	5% from reserves
1964	5%	5% from reserves
1965	5%	5% from reserves

PRICES PAID FOR SHIPS

The following may be of interest to readers, on the subject of costs and their ever upwards climb.

Ship	Bought	Cost	Sold	Fate	Price
Joan Taylor	1858	£2,200			Not recorded
La Plata	1863	£6,511	1872		£3,750
Colorado	1865	£9,200		Foundered	
Concordia (I)	1881	£44,700	1909		£4,300
Alcides	1886	£47,873	1909		£4,900
Warwick**	1889	£29,817	1898	(Wreckage)	$125
Hestia**	1893	£31,580		Foundered	
Kastalia (I)	1897	£47,380	1916		£90,000
Parthenia (I)	1901	£88,920		Torpedoed	
Athenia (I)	1904	£100,967		Torpedoed	
Athenia (II)	1923	£1,250,000		Torpedoed	
Calgaria**	1956	£671,000			Not recorded

**Second Hand Tonnage

Appendix 2: LETITIA (I)

In 1912, just prior to the Great War, the Donaldson Line took delivery of the LETITIA (I) from Scotts' Shipbuilding & Engineering Co. Ltd., of Greenock. She was a twin screw, triple expansion engined vessel of 8,991 tons gross, with a speed of 14 knots. Built for the Canadian service, this ship could carry 300 second and 950 steerage passengers and could comfortably make the passage from Glasgow to the first port, Quebec, in nine days.

Soon after the outbreak of war the LETITIA (I) was taken over as a hospital ship and saw service mainly in the Mediterranean and Atlantic.

On the 1st August, 1917, when repatriating a large number of wounded Canadian troops, she grounded near Chebucto Head, Halifax, Nova Scotia. There was no loss of life among passengers, patients or medical staff. Unfortunately one crew member lost his life. The safe departure from the stranded vessel was attributed to the strict discipline maintained with military passengers.

CORRIENTES *National Maritime Museum*

Appendix 3: CORRIENTES (I)

On the 16th of May 1937 the CORRIENTES (I) was bound up the Thames, in early morning fog patches, from Vancouver to the King George V Dock in London. Shortly before 0700 she collided with the Bullard King vessel UMTALI 8,140 tons which was bound for South Africa. The collision, which occurred off Greenhithe, resulted in the CORRIENTES having a 20 ft. hole torn in her port side in way of the boiler room where a greaser Mr. Charles Mumford was seriously injured and died soon after. The UMTALI suffered extensive bow damage.

After the collision the CORRIENTES was pushed onto a sandbank by six tugs until the damage had been fully assessed and the danger of sinking in the navigation channel averted. The UMTALI was towed to Tilbury for repairs.

The Master, Captain Mathew McKirdie Brown, was found liable at the court of inquiry in June 1937 but appealed and the judgement was altered to 50/50 in 1938. Captain Brown continued with Donaldson Line until his retirement in 1951. He was appointed an O.B.E. in the 1946 New Years Honours List.

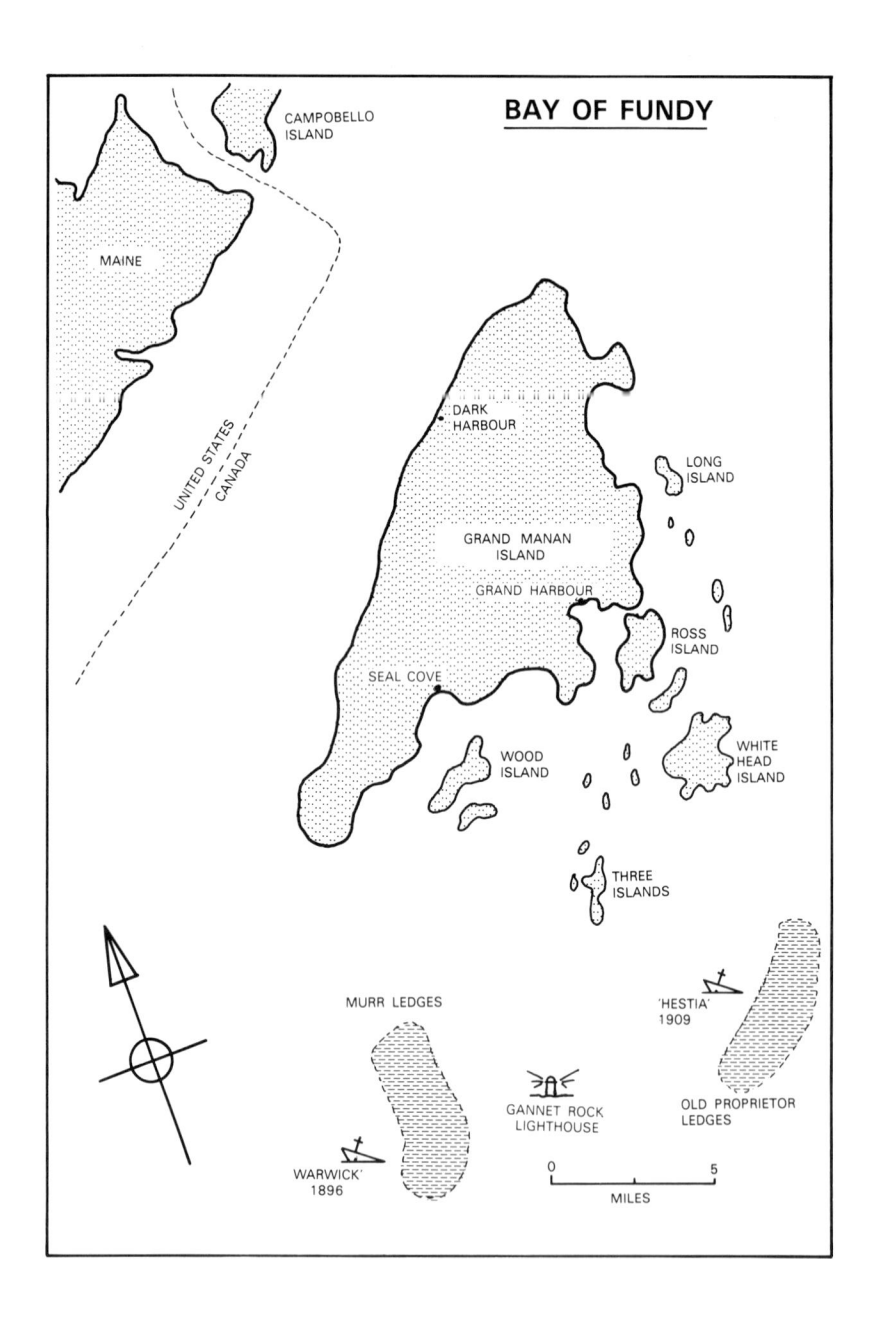

BAY OF FUNDY

- CAMPOBELLO ISLAND
- MAINE
- UNITED STATES / CANADA
- DARK HARBOUR
- LONG ISLAND
- GRAND MANAN ISLAND
- GRAND HARBOUR
- ROSS ISLAND
- SEAL COVE
- WOOD ISLAND
- WHITE HEAD ISLAND
- THREE ISLANDS
- MURR LEDGES
- 'HESTIA' 1909
- GANNET ROCK LIGHTHOUSE
- OLD PROPRIETOR LEDGES
- 'WARWICK' 1896

0 — 5 MILES

Appendix 4: GRAND MANAN ISLAND and the BAY OF FUNDY

Ten miles east of the Maine coast lies Grand Manan Island in the Bay of Fundy. This island comes under the administration of Charlotte County, New Brunswick, and is a notorious place for shipwrecks. From the early 19th century to the 1920s over 150 vessels were wrecked on Grand Manan and the adjacent shoals and islets. The bay is renowned for its world record breaking tides and currents, severe weather and long spells of reduced visibility. On the 30th December, 1896 the WARWICK, bound for St. John, N.B. from Glasgow, grounded on Yellow Ledge, one of the Murr Ledges lying to the south of Grand Manan Island. The following day the crew abandoned ship and were picked up by a fishing schooner from Gloucester, Mass. Considering the deteriorating weather conditions, with a severe north-east gale blowing with snow and reduced visibility, the crew were fortunate to survive.

Much of the WARWICK's cargo was washed ashore on the island and was salvaged by local fishermen. As the cargo contained a large consignment of Scotch Whisky, Grand Manan was not part of the "Dry Belt" that winter.

It is reputed that the total losses amounted to $55,000 for ship and cargo but as was the normal Donaldson practice, she was fully insured. The Receiver of Wrecks eventually disposed of the WARWICK to scrap merchants for $125, the vessel now being in two sections with a large piece of the forward section missing.

On the 25th October, 1909, 13 years after the loss of the WARWICK, the HESTIA, also bound for St. John from Glasgow, grounded on the rocks of Old Proprietor Ledges, south-east of Grand Manan Island. With gale force winds, heavy seas and low temperatures, the HESTIA was taking a heavy pounding on the rocks which forced the Master to give the order to abandon ship. During this operation two boats were smashed and many lives were lost, both passengers and crew. The remaining two boats, once launched, vanished into the night. The six crew remaining aboard crawled to the higher parts of the ship where a long and harrowing wait was to follow.

Their distress signals were unseen on the island mainly due to Thanksgiving celebrations and preparations for the approaching Hallo'een festivities. The day following the grounding, 26th October, someone at Seal Cove spotted the distant wreck. The alarm was raised and numerous boats set out to assist. Thirty-six hours after stranding the six survivors were taken off the HESTIA with considerable difficulty as the swell was very heavy and the ship had started to break up. The schooners ETHEL and DREADNAUGHT each picked up three survivors, both being assisted by the MIZPAH. The crew members were taken to Seal Cove where they were treated with great kindness and compassion.

Over the next few days a frantic effort was made to salvage any undamaged cargo from the HESTIA. On board was a full general cargo including machinery for a battleship under construction in the United States, two prize horses for an American owner and a large consignment of whisky and brandy destined for the Canadian and American markets. The Customs officers were to be kept busy recording the goods salvaged and tracing certain amounts of liquor which had been "washed" ashore and then made its way inland to places of "refuge". After a week the HESTIA slid off the rocks and sank from sight.

During this same week news was received from Nova Scotia that the two lifeboats which got clear of the HESTIA had been found on the shore, one at Yarmouth with three bodies and the other at Port Maitland with one body. A total of 18 victims were recovered in Nova Scotia, including Captain Newman who was Master of the HESTIA. They were all buried at Yarmouth on November 1st, 1909.

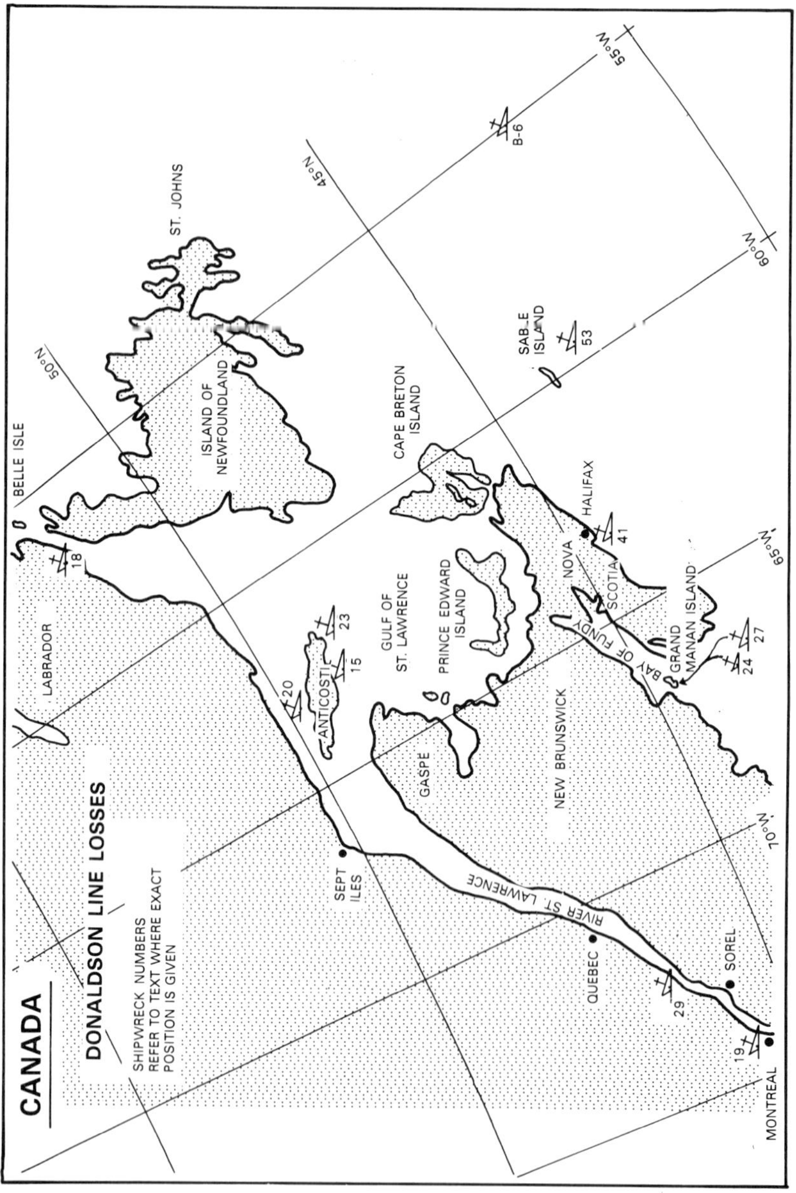
CANADA
DONALDSON LINE LOSSES
SHIPWRECK NUMBERS
REFER TO TEXT WHERE EXACT
POSITION IS GIVEN
LABRADOR
BELLE ISLE
18
50°N
ISLAND OF
NEWFOUNDLAND
ST. JOHNS
45°N
B-6
55°W
60°W
SABLE
ISLAND
53
CAPE BRETON
ISLAND
HALIFAX
41
NOVA
SCOTIA
65°W
GULF OF
ST. LAWRENCE
PRINCE EDWARD
ISLAND
ANTICOSTI
20
23
15
GRAND
MANAN ISLAND
BAY OF FUNDY
24
27
NEW BRUNSWICK
GASPE
SEPT
ILES
RIVER ST. LAWRENCE
70°W
QUEBEC
SOREL
29
19
MONTREAL

At the subsequent inquiry into the stranding it was claimed that the light buoy on Old Proprietor Ledges had been out of order since the Spring of the same year, and this was supported by the Master of an American vessel. The Chief Commissioner of Lights in Ottawa stated the buoy had been operating correctly all summer. Further unexplained questions are: Why was the HESTIA so far west of the usual track to St. John; and why did the Gannet Rock light keepers fail to report the wreck?

This accident was regarded at the time as the worst disaster ever to have occurred in the area.

Appendix 5: ANTICOSTI ISLAND

The Gulf of St. Lawrence is an extensive area of water fed by the River St. Lawrence. To the east lies the island of Newfoundland. Access to and from the Atlantic is by the Strait of Belle Isle to the north and the much wider Cabot Strait to the south.

Anticosti is the large island west of Newfoundland which splits the Gulf in an east-west line. This island is about 140 miles long by 20 miles wide and the name is derived from the Indian term "Natiscosti" meaning "Where bears are hunted".

It is estimated that from the 18th century to recent times a total of 400 ships have been wrecked on Anticosti; the remains of some are still visible along the coasts. The total includes the Donaldson ships CYBELE lost in 1880 and the CIRCE in 1891. The TITANIA which grounded in 1886, was abandoned to the insurers, who salvaged her almost a year later.

In 1895 the French "Chocolate" millionaire M. Henri Menier purchased the island for sport and hunting activities. He built the harbour "Port Menier" at the western end of the island and the remains of his burned down mansion could be seen until recently.

Being in a strategic position in the Gulf, a group of German business men attempted to buy the island in 1938 with a plan to develop a forest product industry and, no doubt, with other objectives in mind. This offer was flatly refused by a very alarmed Canadian Government.

Today the island is primarily a timber producing area, a seasonal hunting ground for sportsmen and an area with a wide variety of bird and marine mammal life.

Appendix 6: CONCORDIA (II) and Sable Island

When on passage from St. John N.B. via Halifax N.S. to Glasgow the CONCORDIA (II) was in collision with the American steamer BLACK EAGLE (ex TOMALVA). The date was 5th March 1934.

The collision occurred about 40 miles south-east of Sable Island, a notorious spit of sand lying towards the southern edge of Sable Bank and about 200 miles east of Halifax N.S.

The CONCORDIA had on board a general cargo and some cattle and horses. She sank shortly after the collision but all the crew of 40 were picked up by the BLACK EAGLE and landed at an Eastern Seaboard port.

Sable Island is approximately $2\frac{1}{2}$ miles by 1 mile, crescent shaped and lies roughly in an East-West line. It has long been known as the Graveyard of the Atlantic having claimed over 200 wrecks, many of the remains still being visible. The lighthouse was automated in the 1960s but the island maintains a weather station manned by Canadian Government staff. Also living on the island is a herd of about 300 wild ponies which survived a shipwreck many years ago. During severe winter conditions it has been known for the R.C.A.F. to fly fodder to Sable Island where it is dropped for the animals.

This island is slowly building up in a North East direction and eroding at the West end. Over the last 200 years it has halved in area and on two occasions the lighthouse has had to be re-positioned.

Appendix 7: LOSS OF THE TRITONIA (III)

On the 28th of February 1929, the TRITONIA was working cargo at the anchorage within the port of Buenaventura, when a fire broke out in the engineroom. This resulted in the ship blowing up due to the fire reaching the cargo of explosives and hazardous goods. An attempt was made to scuttle the ship but this was too late and the two engineers attempting to save the situation lost their lives. Many years later the government and inhabitants proposed that a permanent memorial should be erected in recognition of the heroic deed carried out by the two members of the crew of the TRITONIA.

The following extracts quoted from the Colombian press give a graphic account of the accident and the proposed recognition and respect to the British engineers involved.

Cali, Jueves 17 de Enero de 1985 (Cali, Thursday 17th Jan., 1985)
Dos heroes que salvaron a Buenaventura. Por Alfonso Molina Potes.
(Two heroes who saved Buenaventura. By Alfonso Molina Potes)

On the afternoon of Thursday 28th February, 1929, two officers of the British Merchant Navy sacrificed their lives in action above and beyond the call of duty to save Buenaventura from total destruction.

That morning the 15,000 inhabitants of that port knew about the fire on the TRITONIA. It was a British ship anchored 1,000 metres from the docks. People took it as a spectacle which could be seen very comfortably from the coast in spite of the presence of dynamite in the holds. The ship, which was under the command of Captain Robert White, was carrying 5,500 cases of dynamite, 100 cases of gunpowder, 15,000 detonators, 100 barrels of petrol and 300 tons of other inflammable materials.

At one o'clock in the afternoon Captain White and the crew landed to ask the port authorities for assistance, they were not involved at this time and did not have the equipment or personnel to deal with the situation. There were embarrassed faces when the British asked for help from the rescue boat CARABOBO which was at anchor with its engines out of action for a month. Finally the Chief Engineer Mr. Johnson and the Second Engineer Mr. Hall volunteered to go to the TRITONIA, open the valves and sink it in the bay in a desperate attempt to save the city. They refused all help and, without fear of their fate, the officers boarded the ship. The crowd ashore watched the ship sinking quickly which meant the Britishers had fulfilled their objectives. Soon they were seen on board, calling for help from a rescue craft. When they knew the tragedy was coming they wanted to get off the ship but it was too late. They held hands and were blown up with their ship.

It was four o'clock in the afternoon. The explosion caused a great wave and a great wind which sank six cargo lighters, damaging the sailing vessel SAN ALFONSO, also damaging buildings, windows, doors etc. ashore. Also the spectators were thrown to the ground. Then hysteria came, people were running, shouting that the explosion in the second hold would cause a catastrophe. False rumours took many people to the naval town of Cordoba. Like the mushroom cloud of an atomic explosion the dark cloud covered the sky which went dark. The sun went red, pieces of flaming iron were falling in the streets with a sound like bullets. An officer was hit by one of them and died instantly. The water in the bay turned white from hundreds of dead fish brought to the surface.

The remains of the TRITONIA, which sank in shallow water could be seen until recently.

Captain White and the 37 crew were taken to prison to establish responsibility. In the face of public opinion which accused the authorities of negligence and wished to honour the two officers who gave their lives for the sake of Buenaventura they were released and allowed to go home to their country. (Captain White and three of his officers remained until the enquiry. The rest of the crew travelled overland to Colon where they took passage to the United States then onwards to their home country).

Further press coverage on the disaster was published on Saturday 26th January 1985.

"Three deaths and several injuries were the result of the explosion. The victims were among the curious who had dressed in white suits and hats, almost like going to a party, to come and see the catastrophe. When the echo of the explosion died away it looked like the sun was falling in hot drops to melt the roofs of the houses. A month later some fishermen and primitive divers pulled up in their nets, when fishing in front of the Playa de La Muerte, a life-size Spanish Christ, carved in cedar and with his crystal eyes intact. This was supposed to have been taken to the church in Jacksonville.

The fishermen did not say it was a miracle because the nets also carried Remington Rand typewriters, English bicycles and sewing machines".

The Newspaper of the Port ("El Diario del Puerto") in its edition of 2nd March, 1929 stated "The victims of this deplorable incident deserve the title of heroes as they saved the lives of 15,000 inhabitants by sacrificing their own. Let us revere the names of these sailors, sons of old England".

The Colombian Government's intention to honour the two heroes of the TRITONIA disaster was reported in the local press as follows on Wednesday, 16th January 1985.

"The President, Belisario Betancur, sanctioned Law No. 11 which sets out the means by which a memorial was to be instigated. This Memorial, as the articles below show, was to incorporate both the TRITONIA heroes and the old Colombian Naval vessel called ANDAGOYA.

Article One: The Nation pays tribute to the British officers, Alexander Johnson and William Hall, whose heroic actions in giving their lives to save Buenaventura and the associated homage the Pacific coast gives to the ship ANDAGOYA of the National Fleet.

Article Two: In the development of paragraphs 17 and 22 of the Article 76 of the Political Constitution of Colombia. The National Government will build in the city of Buenaventura the following works which will be integrated in one architectural complex.
a. Auditorium for conventions with all facilities.
b. Installation for the Pacific Naval Museum.
c. Placing the A.R.C. ANDAGOYA in permanent position as a memorial monument. Paragraph. On the hull of the ANDAGOYA there will be a metal plaque with the following inscription:
   THE NATION PAYS TRIBUTE IN RECOGNITION AND ADMIRATION OF THE BRAVE BRITISH NAVAL OFFICERS WHO SACRIFICED THEIR LIVES TO SAVE BUENAVENTURA AND WILL FOR EVER EVOKE GRATEFULNESS IN THE MEMORIES.

Article Three: The National Government through the Minister of Work and Education and the correspondent institutes, will co-ordinate and look after the fulfilment of these works.

MONTREAL

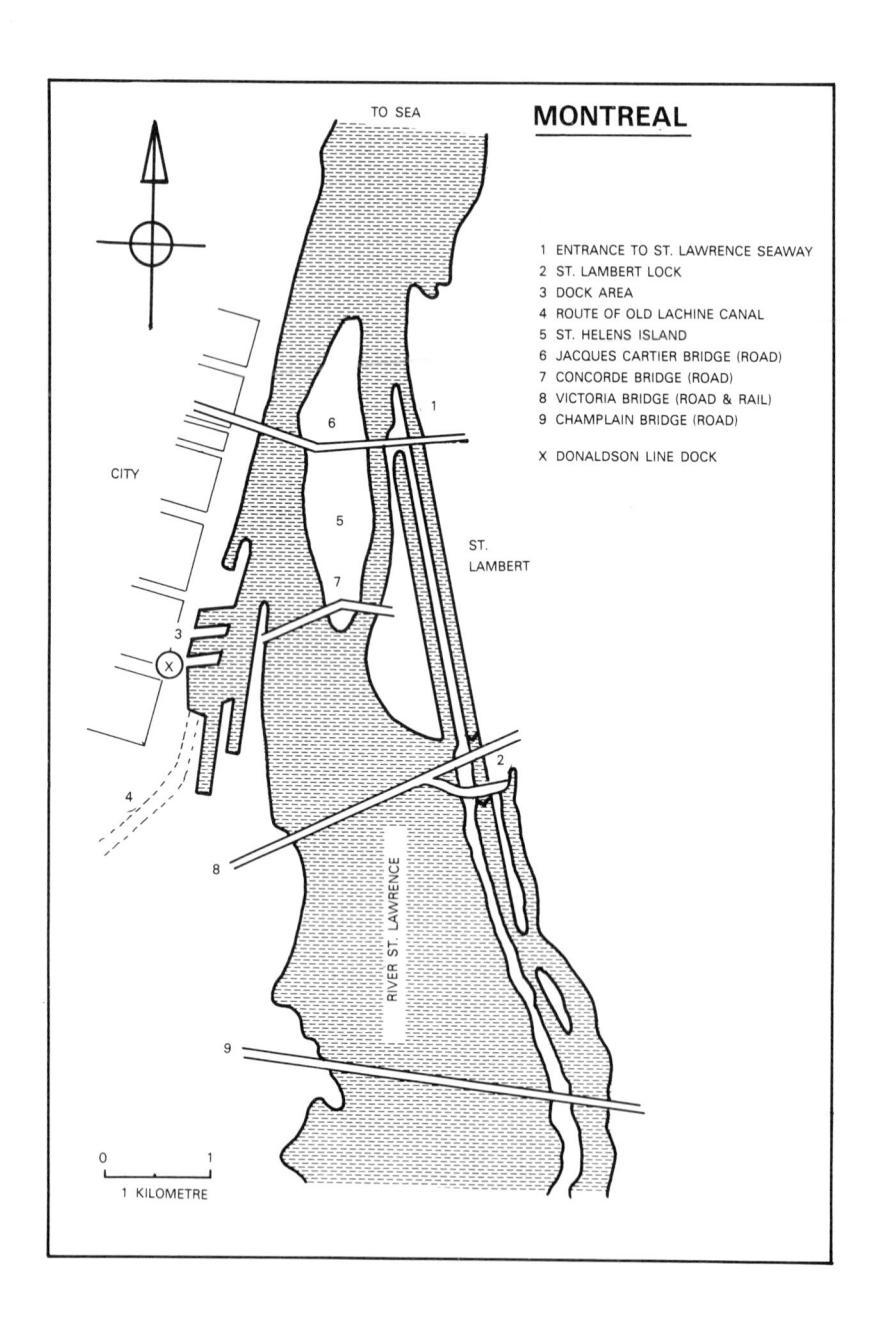

1 ENTRANCE TO ST. LAWRENCE SEAWAY
2 ST. LAMBERT LOCK
3 DOCK AREA
4 ROUTE OF OLD LACHINE CANAL
5 ST. HELENS ISLAND
6 JACQUES CARTIER BRIDGE (ROAD)
7 CONCORDE BRIDGE (ROAD)
8 VICTORIA BRIDGE (ROAD & RAIL)
9 CHAMPLAIN BRIDGE (ROAD)

X DONALDSON LINE DOCK

Appendix 8: THE ST. LAWRENCE SEAWAY SYSTEM

Agreements were signed between the United States and Canada in 1954 and the St. Lawrence Seaway construction commenced. This massive civil engineering project was completed and ships were transiting the system by 1959.

For many years ships had been able to navigate beyond Montreal to the Great Lakes by using the Lachine Canal, which by-passed the St. Lawrence rapids, waterfalls and rock strewn stretches of the upper river. The problem with this route had been the size limitation put on ships, which was about 1,200 tons.

The new seaway allowed ships of much greater size access to the lakes and conversely, the land-locked lake ships were now able to have access to Montreal, Quebec and other ports in the St. Lawrence basin.

DELILIAN passing under the Jacques Cartier Bridge, Montreal, before the creation of the Seaway   *Scottish Maritime Museum*

The St. Lawrence Seaway construction and design was based on the Welland Canal System. This canal, opened in 1929 and the fourth to be built in this vicinity, allowed ships to scale the Niagara Escarpment thus by-passing the Niagara River and its famous falls and providing a route between Lake Ontario and Lake Erie. From the western end of Lake Erie, by using the Detroit River (which is the busiest stretch of navigable water in the world – even surpassing the Dover Straits) and St. Clair River, large ocean going ships could now reach Lake Huron and Lake Michigan. Then, by using the facilities of the canal at Sault Ste. Marie, known as the Soo Locks, which by-passes the St. Mary River Rapids, ships were able to reach Lake Superior and could proceed west to Duluth and Fort William. On arrival at Duluth a ship had climbed 600 feet above sea level and travelled a distance of more than 2,000 miles from the Atlantic.

This canal system allowed general cargo to be moved from Europe, Japan and other locations directly to the mid-west industrial and agricultural areas of Ohio, Illinois, Wisconsin, Michigan and Minnesota, not forgetting the

THE GREAT LAKES

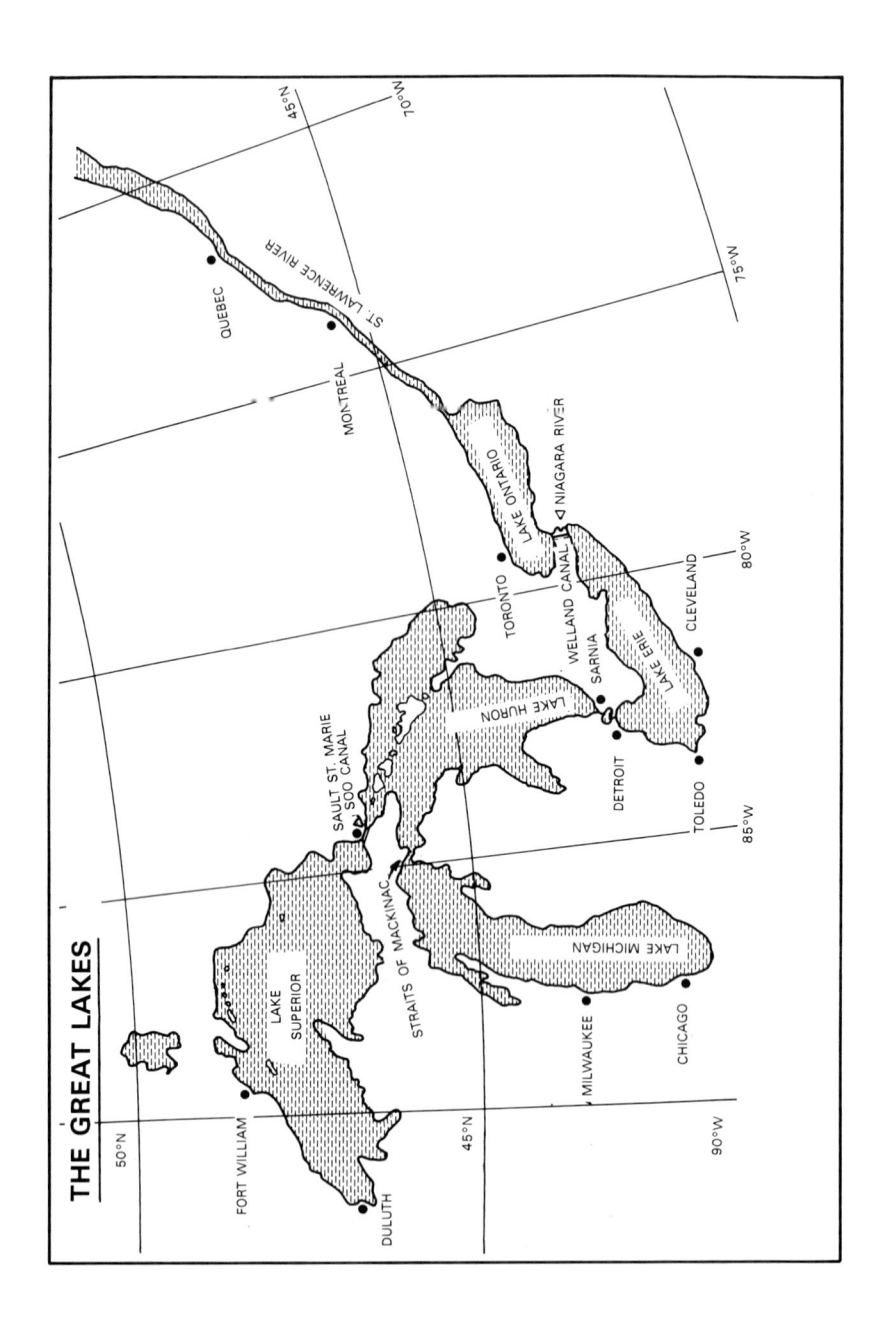

THE GREAT LAKES & ST. LAWRENCE
(IN PROFILE)

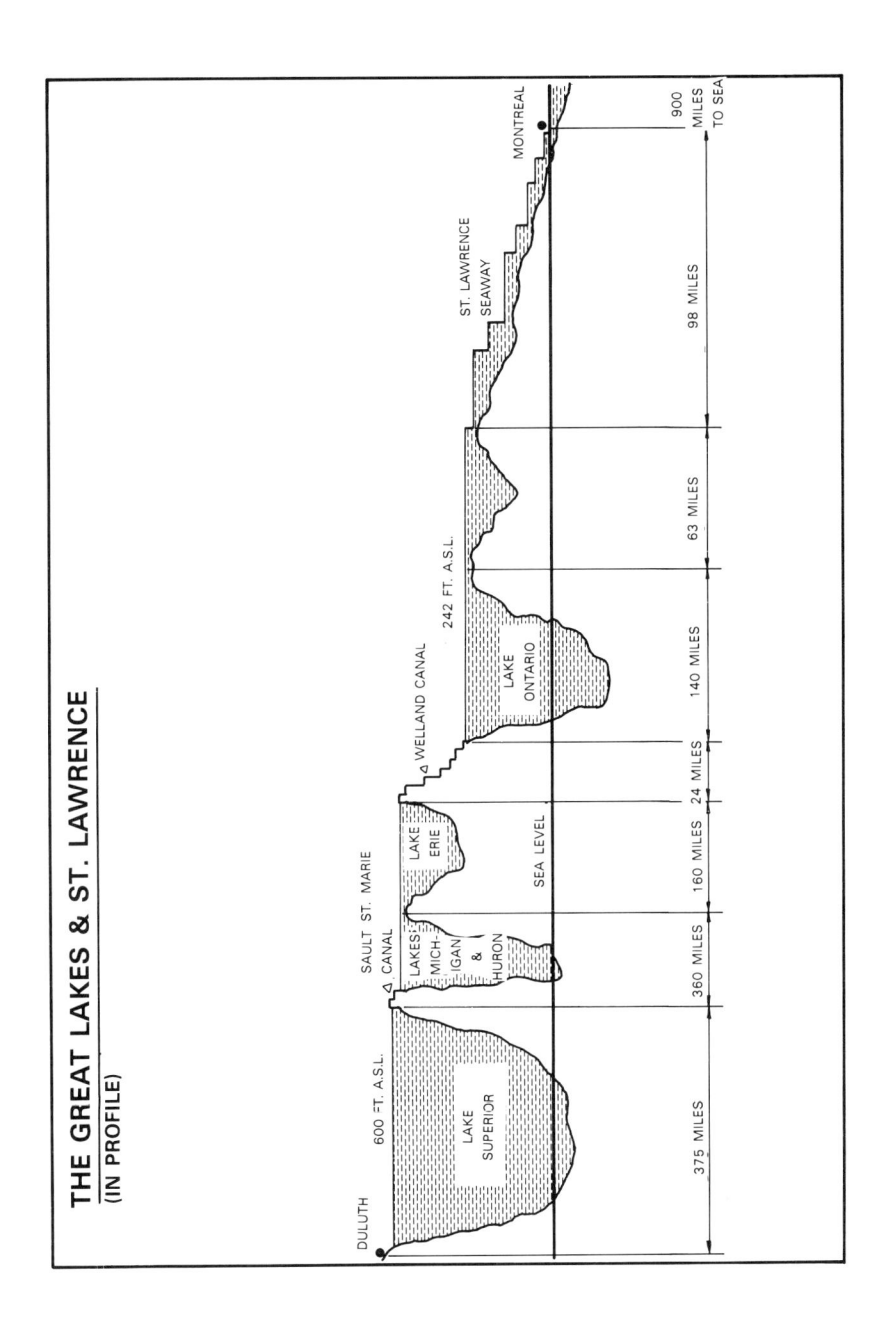

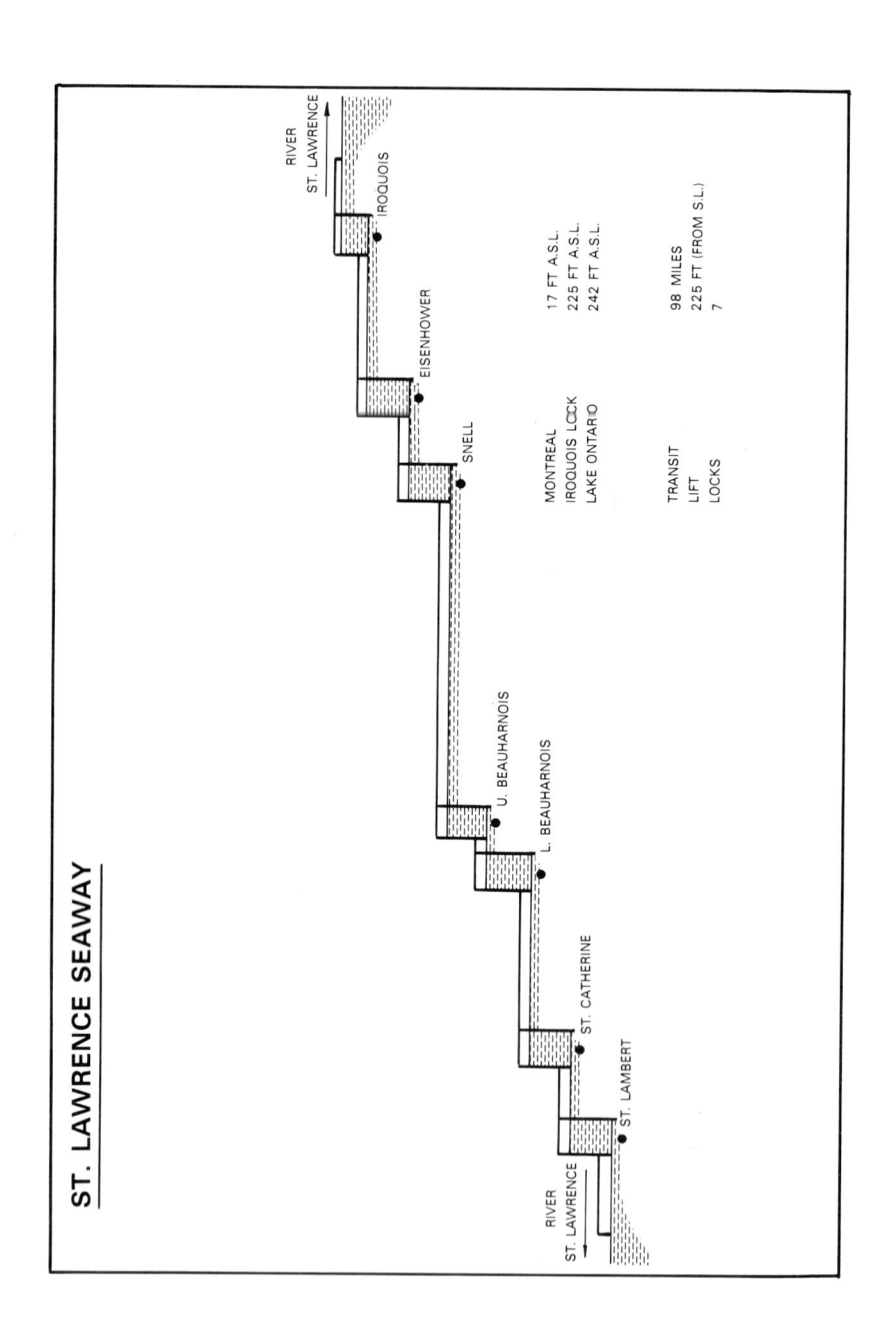

ST. LAWRENCE SEAWAY

- ST. LAMBERT
- ST. CATHERINE
- L. BEAUHARNOIS
- U. BEAUHARNOIS
- SNELL
- EISENHOWER
- IROQUOIS

RIVER ST. LAWRENCE

RIVER ST. LAWRENCE

MONTREAL
IROQUOIS LOCK 17 FT A.S.L.
LAKE ONTARO 225 FT A.S.L.
              242 FT A.S.L.

TRANSIT   98 MILES
LIFT   225 FT (FROM S.L.)
LOCKS   7

WELLAND CANAL

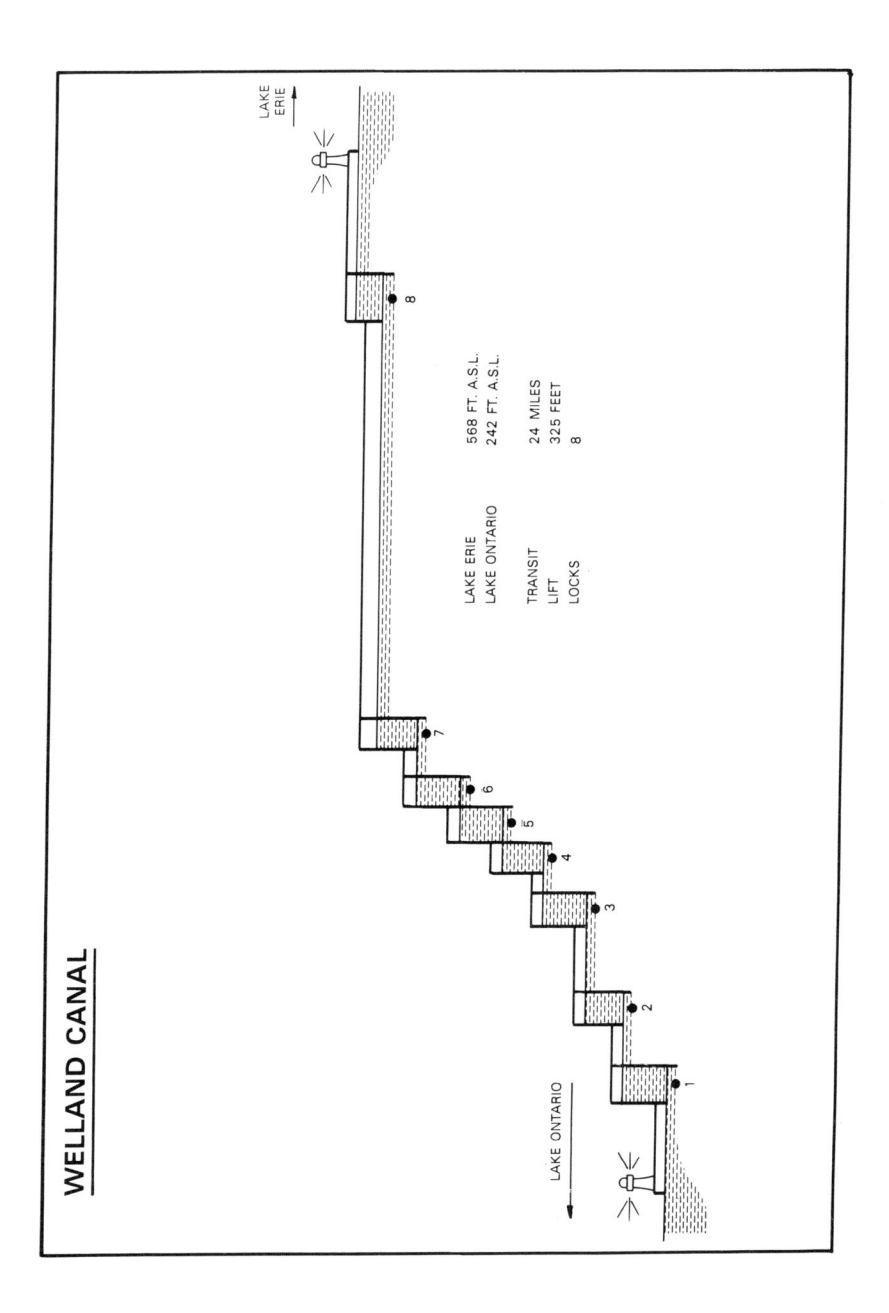

LAKE ERIE	568 FT. A.S.L.
LAKE ONTARIO	242 FT. A.S.L.
TRANSIT	24 MILES
LIFT	325 FEET
LOCKS	8

LAKE ERIE

LAKE ONTARIO

PANAMA CANAL SYSTEM

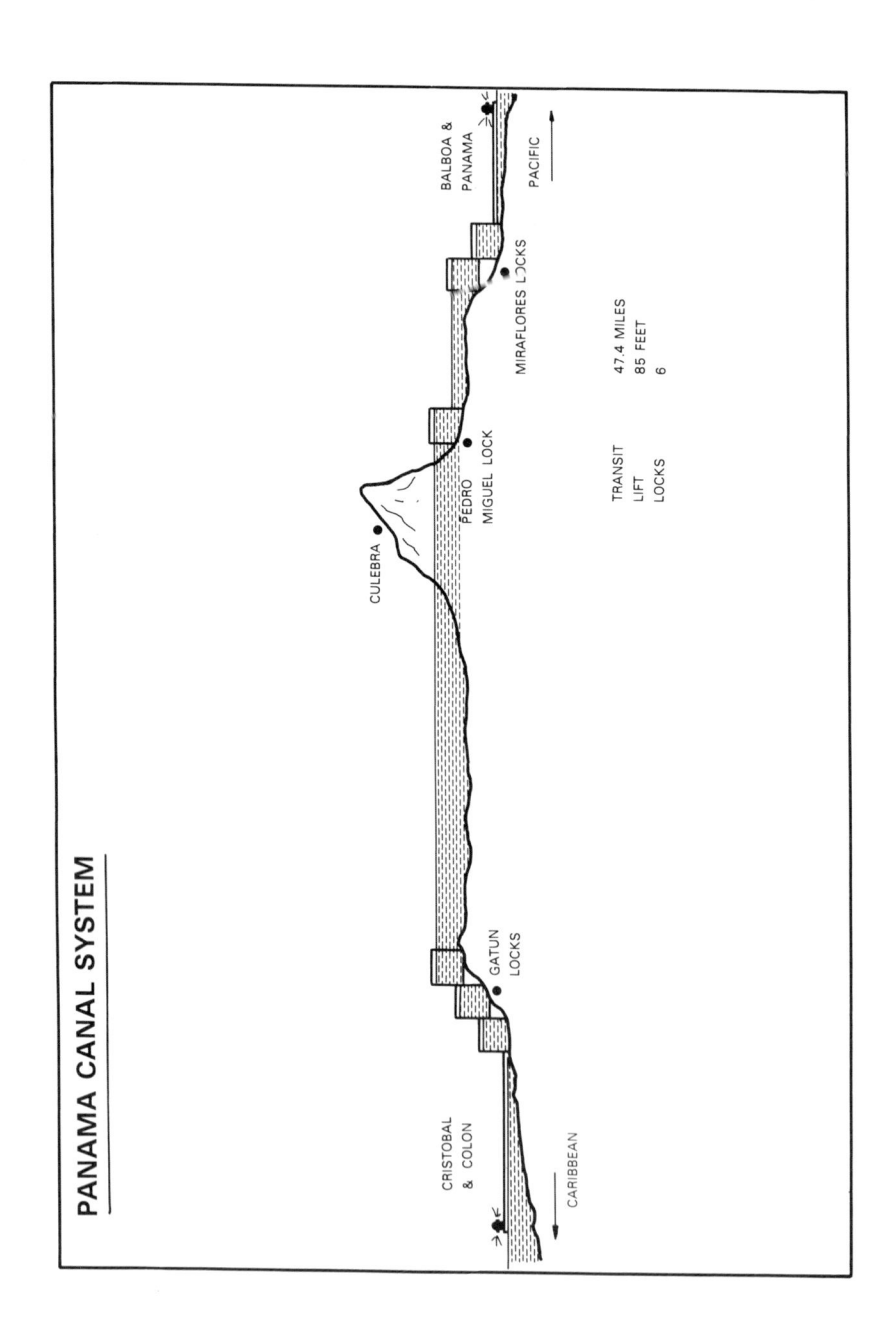

CRISTOBAL & COLON

CARIBBEAN

GATUN LOCKS

CULEBRA

PEDRO MIGUEL LOCK

MIRAFLORES LOCKS

BALBOA & PANAMA

PACIFIC

TRANSIT 47.4 MILES
LIFT 85 FEET
LOCKS 6

Canadian ports of Toronto, Hamilton, Windsor etc. The prime reason for construction of the St. Lawrence Seaway was to allow the large lake vessels to haul bulk grain from the mid-west to places such as Montreal and Quebec and to return loaded with iron ore from Sept Iles, the large ore port at the southern end of the relatively new "Quebec, North Shore and Labrador Railway". This ore is taken directly to the steel foundries and automobile manufacturers in ports such as Cleveland, Toledo and Detroit.

Although the canals were constructed primarily for the United States and Canadian traffic it was inevitable that the world's shipping should find it useful. Donaldson Line was one among many companies that traded the length of the Great Lakes to the heart of this great continent.

Interesting statistics

The locks in the St. Lawrence Seaway and Welland Canal system can accommodate the largest lake ship with some room to spare. These ships are 730 feet overall length by 75 feet beam and a canal draught of 27 feet. The locks in general are over 800 feet long by 80 feet wide; some exceed this length by as much as 400 feet such as Lock 8 in the Welland Canal and the Poe Lock in the Soo Canal. The lift varies considerably from lock to lock, the greatest being at Snell Lock in the St. Lawrence Seaway, N.Y. which has a lift of 46-49 feet, while at Lock 8 in the Welland or the Iroquois Lock in the Seaway the lift can vary from 2-3 feet up to 10 feet depending on the level of the lake and the weather conditions at the time.

To compare with the Panama Canal, completed in 1914, the height of the total lift is only 85 feet at Panama compared to the 600 feet to the Great Lakes although Panama can accommodate larger vessels as the locks are 1,000 feet by 110 feet and the maximum draught is in the region of 45 feet.

Both systems are civil engineering triumphs and are a credit to the thousands involved in their construction. Both are operated to a very high level of efficiency and safety.

Appendix 9: CALGARIA

The CALGARIA was eastbound on her maiden voyage for the Donaldson Line in April 1956 when she came close to foundering. Had she done so, she would have been another mystery of the sea.

After safely docking at Swansea she started unloading the first part of her general cargo, and it was discovered that the arrival draft was in the region of 12 inches more than the departure draft recorded in Canada! (Normally one would expect it to be about 10 inches lighter.) All bilges, cofferdams and empty spaces were checked, but as these continued to show dry soundings, it was a complete puzzle.

The CALGARIA departed Swansea to continue discharging at Avonmouth. Here the mystery was solved. On completion of discharging no. 3 lower 'tween deck, the hatch covers were removed from the top of the orlop deck, the consignment of woodpulp in bales below was barely visible due to serious flooding. The City of Bristol Fire Service was called to pump out the water. Discharging then continued. A consignment of bulk linseed under the wood pulp had formed a crust about a foot thick at its base. This "seal" had saved a consignment of wheat which was stowed below and had prevented the water from both damaging the wheat and reaching the bilges.

When all the cargo had been discharged the ship was laid up. It took a further week to discover the cause of the flooding. A small hole was found in an obsolete drain pipe. In addition, the operational capabilities of the storm valve on this pipe left a lot to be desired. All pipes in this orlop deck were then moved up to the lower 'tween deck and the resulting apertures were plated over and welded.

CALGARIA as the troopship **EMPIRE PRIDE**   Author's collection

Appendix 10: CHARTERED TONNAGE

As noted on page 40, when Donaldson Line entered the Great Lakes trade in 1957 they initially chartered a number of smaller vessels with which to develop the service. Two of these vessels were photographed by Mr. G. E. Langmuir.

ELISABETH HENDRIK FISSER, off Dunglass

RAMPART, off Greenock

Appendix 11: FLAGS AND FUNNEL COLOURS

On ordering their first steamer, the Donaldson Brothers had to decide on a colour for the funnel of the ASTARTE and of the steamers to follow. There are many stories as to why they chose red, white and black but no official record is available. On dropping the titles Clyde Line of Packets and Clyde Line of Steamers around 1880 the funnel colours were changed to black with a broad white band and this remained the colour right up to the voluntary liquidation in 1967.

The Donaldson Line flag is the only design used throughout the company's life and was a rectangular flag with vertical red, white and blue bands of equal width, red to the hoist. Within the white was positioned a black capital "D". The Donaldson Atlantic Line flew the same flag and in addition there was a white pennant with a red and green thistle flown superior to the Donaldson flag. Donaldson South American Line flew in the same position a blue pennant with the letters D.S.A.L. in white.

Anchor-Donaldson Limited flew the Anchor Line house flag on the foremast while the Donaldson flag flew at the main. The Anchor Line flag was (and is) a swallow tail white flag with an inverted anchor and chain in red.

121

DOVER HARBOUR
FIRST WORLD WAR 1914-1918

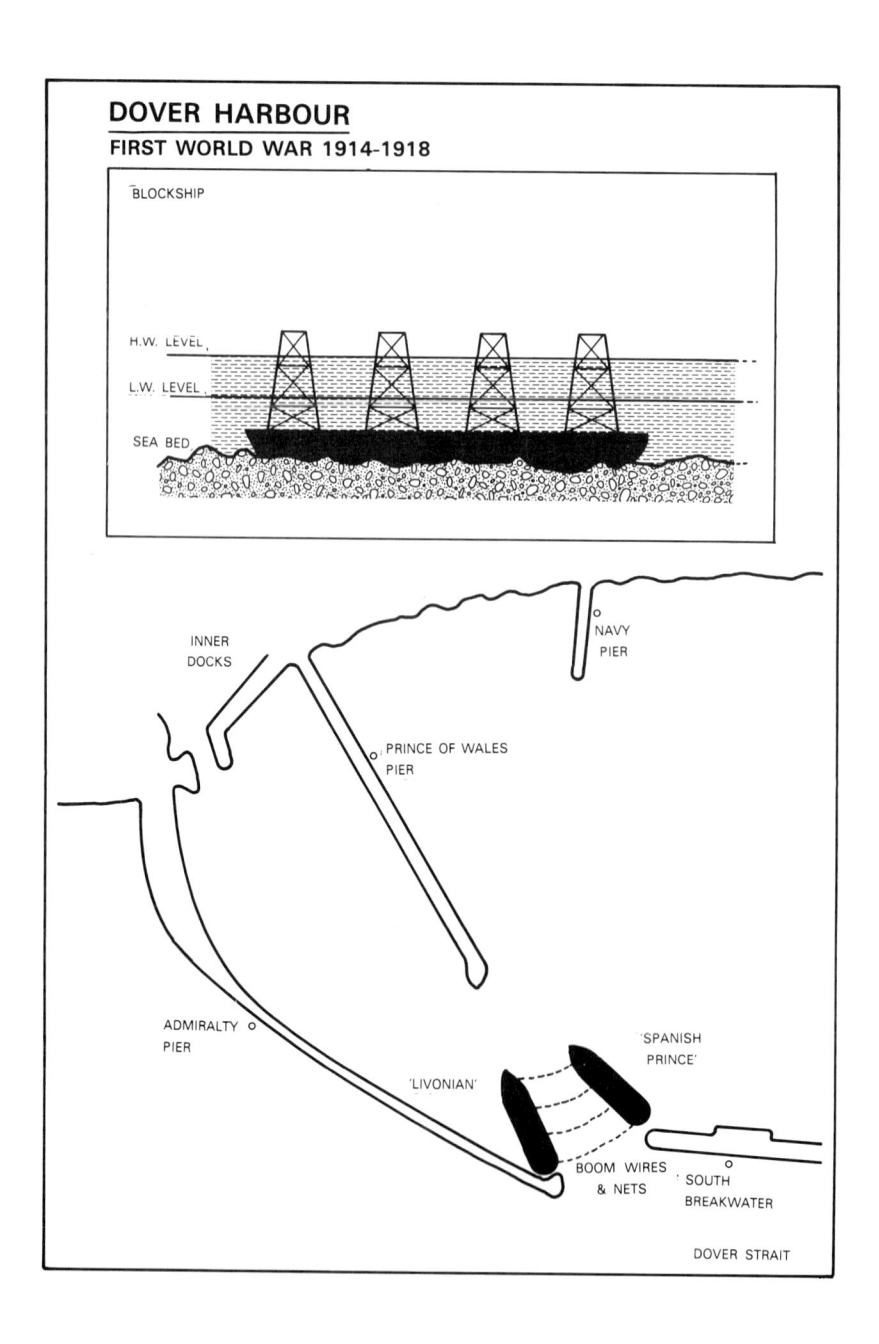

BLOCKSHIP

H.W. LEVEL
L.W. LEVEL
SEA BED

INNER DOCKS

NAVY PIER

PRINCE OF WALES PIER

ADMIRALTY PIER

'LIVONIAN'

'SPANISH PRINCE'

BOOM WIRES & NETS

SOUTH BREAKWATER

DOVER STRAIT

Appendix 12: THE LIVONIAN AS A BLOCKSHIP AT DOVER

As readers will note in the ship detail section, the LIVONIAN was under Donaldson Line control for a very brief period before being sold to the Admiralty for use as a blockship.

The LIVONIAN and another vessel the SPANISH PRINCE were taken to Dover by the Navy where both had their funnels, masts and upper decks removed. The hull was then cut down to a height where the remaining uppermost deck would be about 10 feet below the surface of the water at Low Water Springs. On top of the hulks steel pylons were constructed to enable wires and nets to be suspended between the ships thus protecting the harbour entrance from submarine attack. Both ships were then filled with Thames gravel and the delicate task of sinking them was carried out by the Navy. The LIVONIAN was in position in December 1914 and the SPANISH PRINCE in March 1915.

Many years later it was decided to raise the LIVONIAN as she was closest to the Admiralty Pier thus bringing the western entrance back into use for packet boats etc. Dover Harbour Board received no suitable tender for the work so it was decided to carry out the task with their own staff under the directions of the Harbour Master. This complex operation commenced in February 1931. The hulk was cut into sections and raised by lighters using six 9 inch steel wires attached to the wreck after channels 45 ft. × 5 ft. × 6 ft. were cut in the chalk and flint under the wreck. Two sections of 1,500 tons each were raised and towed off for scrap. The remaining pieces were dynamited where they lay.

After a two year operation with 40 men and six divers the Western Entrance was declared clear for navigation on the 6th May 1933.

The SPANISH PRINCE remained where she lay but the pylons were removed and after numerous ships struck the wreck it was decided to place a light buoy over her bow. The remains of this wreck are still buried in the mud today where she settled in 1915.

Appendix 13: MERCHANT NAVY WAR MEMORIAL

Many merchant seamen who lost their lives in two World Wars have no graves other than the sea itself. There are two memorials situated in Trinity Gardens, Tower Hill, London. The memorial for those killed in the 1914-1918 War takes the form of a classic arcade with eight columns arranged in four pairs. The ships represented on this memorial are listed on plates attached to the faces of the columns.

Across a small lawn is situated the memorial to those who perished in the 1939-1945 War. This is in the form of a sunken garden with seats and rose beds. The walls enclosing this area have the plates secured to them, again in alphabetical order as shown in the photographs opposite.

The bronze plates have the names of the seafarers set out under the ship they last served on. To assist visitors in the location of names there are framed diagrams of the memorials at each entrance and finding the vessel is quite simple. Should the visitor have difficulty in tracing a seafarer's name, one can consult an alphabetical list of names kept at the offices of Trinity House which is close by. Further information can be obtained from the following establishments:-

Commonwealth War Graves Commission
2 Marlow Road
Maidenhead
Berkshire
SL6 7DX
Tel. 0628 34221

The Registrar-General
Board of Trade
Central Register and Records Office of Shipping and Seamen
Llantrisant Road
Llandaff
Cardiff
S. Wales

It should be noted that the memorials in Trinity Gardens, list the names of registered seafarers only. Passengers, gunners and supernumeraries are not recorded on the memorials.

THE BRITISH MARITIME CHARITABLE FOUNDATION "MEMORIAL BOOK"

The British Maritime Charitable Foundation sponsored a Memorial Book which is on permanent display in the Mariners' Chapel, Church of All Hallows By the Tower, Tower Hill, London.

This book was dedicated in the presence of Countess Mountbatten of Burma (Honorary President of the Foundation) in March 1987. A service of rededication will be held every two years.

The Memorial Book is to commemorate names of those lost at sea, by whatever chance or accident, whose bodies were never recovered and "have no known grave". This is without regard to nationality or creed.

In fact anyone wanting to commemorate a member of their family, or friend who is lost at sea, can do so by applying to:-

The British Maritime Charitable Foundation
25-27 Theobalds Road
London
WC1X 8SP
Tel. 01-405 7488

The Merchant Navy War Memorial 1914-1918, showing the plates on the end pillars

The West Wing of the Merchant Navy War Memorial 1939-1945, showing the plates around the walls

Author's photographs

FLEET LIST INDEX

Names in CAPITALS are those borne by ships when owned or managed by Donaldson; names in lower case type are of the ships when in other ownership.

AIRTHRIA	72	CYBELE	15	Karos	89
Aktian	95	CYNTHIA	19	KASTALIA (I)	31
Al Sudan	B.10	Cutcombe	A.1	KASTALIA (II)	59
ALCIDES	22			Kaukhali	84
ALCONDA	49	DAKOTIAN	78	KEEMUN	30
Almeria Lykes	B.3	DELILIAN	80	Kelvingrove	47
ALMORA	33	DORELIAN	81	Kinaros	92
AMARYNTHIA	25	Drachnstein	38	KIRKHOLM	54
Andrew C. Crosbie	95	DUNACHTON	52		
Anja	72			LA PLATA	4
Ardpatrick	B.9	EIRENE	18	LAKONIA (I)	34
ARGALIA (I)	51	Embassy	93	LAKONIA (II)	88
ARGALIA (II)	55	EMPIRE ARQUEBUS	B.10	LAURENTIA	90
Armathia	59	EMPIRE BARDOLPH	B.8	LETITIA (I)	41
ASTARTE	12	EMPIRE BRENT	69	LETITIA (II)	69
ATHENIA (I)	37	EMPIRE CONDOR	B.3	LETITIA (III)	96
ATHENIA (II)	65	Empire Cromer	84	LISMORIA	91
Attila	45	EMPIRE CURLEW	B.4	LIVONIAN*	42
		Empire Flag	85	Lübeck	72
Bella Scott	‡	EMPIRE KANGAROO	87	Ludgate Hill	42
Bennevis	A.1	EMPIRE PICKWICK	B.9		
Bibi	96	Empire Pride	93	Maldive Trader	94
Borderdale	50	EMPIRE REDSHANK	B.5	Manila	32
Braddock	B.5	EMPIRE SPRING	B.6	MARANON	10
Bransfield	61	Empire Treasure	86	MARGARET	
		EMPIRE WHALE	B.2	FALCONER	3
		Erminia Mazzella	87	Maria	13
CABOTIA (I)	43	ESMOND	75	Maria Elaine	77
CABOTIA (II)	57	Essex Glade	49	MARINA (I)	13
CALGARIA	93	Europa	32	MARINA (II)	35
Cameta	48			MARY	‡
Cape St. Vincent	B.10	Fleetway	‡	Mary Beyts	27
Captain Antonios K.	59	Fleetwood	‡	MARY FALCONER	2
CAPTAIN COOK	69	Florencia	‡	Medina Victory	90
CARMIA (I)	38	Flying Gull	B.4	Memling	B.8
CARMIA (II)	85			Mercer	87
Caruaru	47	GARTSHERRIE	‡	MERCURIA	47
CASSANDRA	38	GERALDINE MARY	67	Merton Hall	25
Caxias	47	GLAMIS CASTLE	23	MIAMI	8
Cedrington Court	57	GRACIA (I)	64	Miyadono Maru	55
CHALISTER	56	GRACIA (II)	86	MODAVIA	70
Charlton Pride	93	GREGALIA	73	MOVERIA	68
CHILIAN	16	GRETAVALE	53		
Cicero (H.M.S.)	B.10	Gulistan	50	Neon	91
CIRCE	23	Gyokuyo Maru	A.1	Ningpo	92
Clan Mackendrick	B.9			NORTONIAN	76
CLUTHA	45	Haggersgate	56	NORWEGIAN	77
COLINA (I)	14	Haringhata	B.9	NUBIAN	79
COLINA (II)	95	HESTIA	27		
COLORADO	7	Hodur	56		
CONCORDIA (I)	21	Holkar	45	OCEAN WANDERER	B.7
CONCORDIA (II)	53			ONTARIAN	43
CORACERO	66	IMUNCINA	9	ORCADIAN	44
CORDILLERA	61	Inchearn	85	Oregon Star	86
CORINALDO (I)	62	Inchleana	86	ORMIDALE	46
CORINALDO (II)	92	Inchmay	84	Ormiston	44
CORRIENTES (I)	60	INDRANI	26	ORTHIA	29
CORRIENTES (II)	84	Ines	47		
CORTONA (I)	63	Istros	46		
CORTONA (II)	89			Paraguay	13
CRANLEY	48	JOAN TAYLOR	1	PARANA	5

126

PARTHENIA (I)	36	SALACIA (II)	52	Traprain Law	75
PARTHENIA (II)	54	SALACIA (III)	82	Trelevan	72
PARTHENIA (III)	87	SAMFINN	B.12	TRITONIA (I)	28
Patricia	30	SAMHORN	B.11	TRITONIA (II)	50
Patrie	30	SAMTRUSTY	88	TRITONIA (III)	58
PERUVIAN	17	Sangaetano	88	Tusker Rock	59
Pina Onorato	87	Santa Irene	B.7		
Po	20	SANTONA (I)	11	URUGUAY	6
POLARIA	44	SANTONA (II)	94		
PYTHIA	39	SATURNIA	40	Vancouver Star	B.8
		Scapa Flow	72	VARDULIA	71
Quarto	32	Sheng Yu	52	Verdun	71
		Slangevecht	3	Victoria Star	85
Raglan Castle	39	Sordello	‡		
Ready	39	SULAIRIA	74	WAR EMU	58
REBECCA	‡	Swanley	51	War Kestrel	55
Regina	9			WAR OSTRICH	A.1
Reina Margarita	9			War Viper	57
Robin Doncaster	B.4	Taos Victory	91	WARWICK	24
ROTHERMERE	83	Tepic	96	Winona County	B.2
Ruysdael	B.7	Tepora	96		
		Tetulia	86	Yonne	31
St. Domingo	39	TITANIA	20		
SALACIA (I)	32	Torero	13	Zuisyo Maru	52

*LIVONIAN No. 42

This vessel passed through Donaldson Line control briefly as part of a deal with Allan Line whereby their ships and the trade rights on the South American services were bought by Donaldson Brothers but the ancient LIVONIAN was not intended to be part of the package, although Allan insisted it was. The matter went to arbitration and Donaldson won the day. The LIVONIAN passed back to Allan Line where she operated for a further brief period on the South American route to complete commitments. In March 1914 she was taken off service and laid up in Gareloch until sold to the Admiralty.

‡See page 92.

NOTES:

Bearing in mind the close relationship between Anglo-Newfoundland Development Company and the Donaldson Line, deep-sea ships owned by the former have been included chronologically in the fleet list.

From the early days of trading to the last few months leading up to liquidation of the company in 1967, Donaldson Line provided limited passenger accommodation on most of their freight ships. This could be for four, six, ten or twelve passengers. The facilities provided were always comfortable and up to date. The mainly passenger units of the fleet carried numbers ranging from fifty-five to well over a thousand and the emphasis was always on steerage and cabin class passengers rather than First Class. Limited accommodation was provided for the latter on the North Atlantic passenger services, on ships such as the SATURNIA, CASSANDRA, LETITIA (I) and (II) and ATHENIA (I) and (II).

Where a Fleet List number appears more than once, this shows the vessel concerned operated under Donaldson Line ownership with more than one name i.e. she was purchased but her existing name was not changed until a later date.

Rear cover illustration: Sunset, Lake Ontario. *Author's photograph*

WORLD SHIP SOCIETY PUBLICATIONS

This is one of a substantial number of shipping company histories published by the World Ship Society. Full details are available from the Society at 52 Nursery Road, Sunderland SR3 1NT. Titles in print at the end of 1989 included:

ALBYN LINE
AUSTRALIAN NATIONAL LINE
BEN LINE, with 1985 Supplement
BLAND GIBRALTAR
CAMBRIAN COASTERS
CHAPMAN OF NEWCASTLE
CONSTANTINE GROUP
CONVERSION FOR WAR
EMPIRE TUGS
FERRY MALTA
FROM AMERICA TO UNITED STATES
   In Four Parts
GAS AND ELECTRICITY COLLIERS
GEORGE GIBSON & CO.
THE GORTHON SHIPPING COMPANIES 1915-1985
HAIN OF ST. IVES
HAMBURG SOUTH AMERICA LINE*
HAMBURG TUGS
HEAD LINE (THE ULSTER STEAMSHIP CO. LTD.)
IDYLL OF THE KINGS (KING LINE)
IRISH SHIPPING LTD.
LONDON & OVERSEAS FREIGHTERS 1949-1977
P&O, A FLEET HISTORY*
SCOTTISH FISHERY PROTECTION
SCRAP AND BUILD
SOVIET PASSENGER SHIPS 1917-1977
WM. SLOAN & CO. LTD. 1825-1968
STAG LINE
STEPHENS, SUTTON LTD.
WEST HARTLEPOOL STEAM NAVIGATION CO. LTD.

Naval Titles:

HUNT CLASS DESTROYERS
IRISH NAVAL SERVICE
THE TYPE 35 TORPEDO BOATS OF THE KRIEGSMARINE
TOWN CLASS DESTROYERS

                              *indicates case-bound